The *Real* Secrets Women Only Whisper

WARNING! WARNING! WARNING!

KEEP THIS BOOK AWAY FROM MEN!

DONNA ESTES ANTEBI

The Real Secrets Women Only Whisper

Manufactured in the United States of America

10 9 8 7 6 5 4 3 2

Library of Congress Cataloging in Publication Data

Antebi, Donna Estes
The Real Secrets Women Only Whisper: Warning Keep This Book Away From Men! / The 21st Century Women's Guide to Success and Survival including the dirty tricks EVERY women needs to know!/You don't have to learn the hard way!/Donna Estes Antebi
p. cm. 2009912398
1. Women 2. Relationships 3. Love 4. Sex 5.Marriage 6. Men 7. Self-Realization
I. Title

ISBN 978-0-9823825-3-0 (hardcover)
ISBN 978-0-9823825-2-3 (e-book)
ISBN 978-0-9823825-4-7 (kindle)
ISBN 978-0-9823825-5-4 (iBook)

Publishing Consultant: DunhamGroupInc.com
Cover Design: DogEaredDesign.com
Interior Design: BlackbirdCreative.biz
Cover Photo: MariaPhotography.com

www.TheRealSecretsWOW.com

Contents

Dedication

To the 21st Century Woman; for between us is an unbreakable bond.
Every struggle one woman has endured, another has survived.
By sharing our truth, we become united by wisdom.

Foreword

BY CHRISTINE PETERS

We all have that one friend. The one constant in our lives that we can always count on to tell us the truth, regardless of circumstances. Donna's been a friend of mine for many years. I would consider her more like a sister. Donna's advice isn't just a philosophy; it's the way she lives her life.

Surviving and thriving in the cutthroat, male-driven world of Hollywood, Donna has been a true inspiration as a successful businesswoman, a philanthropist, loving and supportive mother and the rock of Gibraltar to her husband, Steve. No small feat in a town notorious for its failed marriages, ruined dreams and shattered families.

While reading this book, it dawned on me that Donna was saying everything I always wanted to say. It was the lessons of my own life laid out in front of me. Having had to protect my two young daughters through a difficult public divorce; having survived the "Boys Club" of Hollywood, while balancing the role of motherhood and breadwinner; dealing with the toxic relationships and politics that threatened to block my career and having been gossiped about and dragged through the press, the old saying 'had I known then what I know now' rings true for me every day. It is paramount to me to teach my girls to be independent and help them avoid the same mistakes I've made. I want them to be strong, self-confident and independent – without permission from a man to feel so.

When I produced the movie, "How to Lose a Guy in 10 Days," I intentionally created a role model in Andie Anderson, an unsinkable girl who would inspire women to be fearless in life and love. And now Donna tells you "How-To" do just that and rely on yourself and your own abilities.

As Eleanor Roosevelt once said: "No one can make you feel inferior without your consent," and this book gives you the keys to take control of not only your relationship, but also of your *life,* all while making you laugh along the way!

This book is a true treasure trove. It's the ultimate survival guide and it's our duty as successful women, mothers, and daughters, to share this invaluable advice with each other. With the pressures of the economic downturn and the rollercoaster we ride called *life*, we can sometimes feel like our lives are spiraling out of control. The advice she offers, the secrets she shares, are not just how to find happiness in love, but how to find it in life.

She covers it all: Men. Women. And everything that comes in between.

Introduction

They say that everyone has a natural gift. Mine happens to be coaching people on how to successfully navigate through just about any imaginable course – up the ladder, out the door, down the aisle or off the ledge. After coaching countless women, I discovered that women of all ages are finding themselves increasingly undermined by the forces of a hyper-sexualized media and the unexpected consequences of the 1960s divorce revolution.

Women fought for the right to have it all. Now we have the obligation to do it all. Talk about bitter sweet. Women are way too often forced to fend for their families alone. It is a harsh reality check when studies show that women without children make 90 cents to a man's dollar, married mothers make 73 cents, and single mothers only make 60 cents to a man's dollar! No wonder that same study showed women's happiness levels have declined while men's happiness has increased.

Young women are struggling to find decent suitors through this porn-tainted, silicone-spoiled generation of men. And wives are increasingly being forced into woman-on-woman combat to defend their relationships against the never-ending supply of morally challenged women ("Weeds" as I refer to them) who are trying to set double-D-sized booby traps to catch the wandering eyes of wayward husbands. Women on the far side of hot flashes are having to enter into survival mode in order to co-exist with a nation full of aging, fountain-of-youth-seeking men who are knocking back Viagra and fist bumping their motto "What happens in Vegas, stays in Vegas!"

So, how are women supposed to maneuver through the moral minefields of the 21st century? Modern women are asking for help. And that's exactly where this book comes in.

Sharing my woman-to-woman advice with the world was not something I intended to do. It was actually a gradual process that came about quite accidentally after a friend asked if I would have a talk with her daughters as they were preparing to move out of the family home and into their own place. She wanted me to tell them the real secrets every smart woman needs to know and to share with them the brutal truth about subjects that are difficult for a mother to talk about – and even more difficult for daughters to hear about from their mothers. I accepted this honorable task. I took the mission very seriously, and in preparation for our talk, I made notes of things I believed they should know. The more I pondered, the more I realized what a gift it would be if women of all ages could shortcut the learning curve of life by having a real world survival guide with bottom line, topical advice at their fingertips. Now that, I thought, would be a priceless gift! So, my notes shifted from good-girl inspiration to the real-girl, no-holds-barred advice that most women only learn the hard way.

I included in *The Real Secrets Women Only Whisper* every subject imaginable: love, sex, power, men, money, marriage, dating, cheating, divorce, children, friends, enemies, beauty, aging, and every dirty trick in between. I even covered topics the girls might not fully appreciate for another ten, twenty, or even thirty years. I then decided to have the advice printed and bound into a book so they could keep it as a reference guide many years into the future. They were thrilled.

The manuscript was such a hit, that not only did the girls love it, but their mother and grandmother did too. I found that the few extra copies I made for myself were continually being circulated from one friend in crisis to another. My daughter, Lily, and her Kappa Sorority sisters read the book so much they would recite its passages to each other like bible verses.

It was actually actress Heather Locklear who, after entertaining her make-up ladies with the book on a movie set, encouraged me to have it published so that all women could gain a better understanding of how to deal with the collective challenges we face. And so, this is how the book came to be.

The Real Secrets Women Only Whisper is a gift of knowledge accumulated from countless heartaches of generations of women. Some of the most important advice in this book may surprise you, as it is counterintuitive and unconventional – these are the real secrets usually only whispered between the wisest of women to the closest of friends. Some of the advice you will agree with, and some of it you may disagree with completely. One thing I am sure of – in this book you will find at least a secret or two that you will use to change your life for the better.

Hopefully you will, in turn, share the wisdom that resonates with you with the women you care about. It's a tough world out there for women, and we need all the help we can get. Perhaps with a little extra help from each other, fewer women will be looking back with regret whispering to their friends, "If I only knew then what I know now..."

I recommend that if you're presently in a life crisis, you go straight to the section you need. After that, read the whole book and mark the pages you want to refer to and those that you wish to pass on to someone you care about. Then lock the book away from the prying eyes of men. I am not kidding! After reading it, it'll be very clear why I intentionally buried the real secrets in between the pages of everyday wisdom. There is information in this book you can use to your great advantage, and it is better for you (and all women) if men don't know what's inside. (You don't want to give them any ideas they don't already have!)

My hope for all of us is that by sharing our greatest wisdom, we can get on the same page, unite our strengths, support each other and work together to regain some of the ground that has been lost for women in the moral apocalypse of America.

WARNING! WARNING! WARNING!

FRIENDS & ENEMIES

The Devil in Disguise

Everyone is not as nice as you. It's a competitive world on every level, and there's no shortage of mean girls who will kiss you when you walk in the door, then turn around and knife you in the back as you leave.

Not all women are cheerleaders for other women's good fortune. In fact, your good fortune may be a good enough reason for them to try and knock you down a notch or two. The Gayle Kings of the world are few and far between. You will be well-served to learn the difference between a friend who is your champion and a friend who would prefer to keep you in your rightful place – a couple rungs below her on the ladder of success.

Guard yourself professionally and privately from those with the "evil eye." Hold your cards close to your chest and beware of these charming little devils. If they suspect you're up to something that might outshine them, their competitive spirit might compel them to take subversive action by undermining your opportunities, your access and your efforts.

Dark Secrets

If you're going to share your darkest secrets (and hopefully you don't have *too* many!) with a friend, you better be sure this friend has what it takes to be your friend for life. There is nobody more dangerous than a former friend in possession of those secrets. If you aren't sure who to trust and need to talk, share your secrets with a psychologist, and even then, don't use real names.

Girlfriends

Girlfriends can be one of the greatest aspects of your life. Women need girlfriends to talk with and share our experiences, joys, and sorrows with. We need friends to vent our frustrations to and to help keep us centered. Our ability to have close female friends helps us keep our sanity, saves us a fortune in therapy bills and also helps us live longer.

However, women need to understand that all things have a season, including friendships. Some friends are meant to last a lifetime, and some friendships are transitory, based on shared time, close proximity or present commonality of interest. Some friends are there to share in your dating dramas; some are there to share in motherhood; some are there to share in marital bliss or marital woes; some friends are there to wipe your tears; and others are present to encourage business relationships or spiritual growth. Some are there just to help you through a crisis, and some may even be there to remind you of what you don't want in a friend.

All friendships are meant to be. But they're not all meant to be forever – and that's okay. If you can accept that not all friendships are meant to last forever, then you can learn to let go of "friendship expectations" and lessen your disappointment when a natural evolution takes place. Learn to embrace your friendships simply for the joy they bring to your life during the special time you share.

There is great freedom in accepting the ebb and flow of friendships without having to feel insecure or trying to cling to a friendship whose season is coming to an end. You will be much happier if you can trust that everyone is on his or her own journey in life, and that with each friendship that slowly fades away, another will have an opportunity to grow and blossom in its place.

They Don't Hate You Because You're Beautiful

If you ever hear a woman say, "They hate me because I'm beautiful," then you know two things are for sure: one, that this is a woman who doesn't have many female friends, and two, the reason why they hate her has nothing to do with her beauty.

If women hate her, it's usually for a number of legitimate reasons. Maybe she's a liar or a mean-spirited, backstabbing gossip. Maybe she can't be trusted, or maybe she just isn't a "girl's girl." Perhaps she's one of those cunning women who has been known to work her way around the husbands in the room, coyly whispering how her man "just doesn't satisfy her anymore." This is an age-old, yet surprisingly effective ploy frequently used by women who have no girlfriends because "they're all just jealous," of course.

Keep your distance from these self-proclaimed "beautiful" women who everyone supposedly envies. If you find her radar has honed in on your husband at a party, then galvanize your "just jealous" friends in a spontaneous, shoulder-to-shoulder wife block to distract her attention and prohibit her access to the potentially sympathetic ears of the husbands in the room, including yours. (That's what your Gayle King girlfriends are for!)

I know some of you are saying this sounds like the behavior of a jealous, insecure wife. Call it what you like, but it's better to stand your ground as a fiercely territorial wife than an oblivious, soon-to-be ex-wife.

Keep It Between the Sheets

Keep the intimate details of your sex life to yourself. That is, if you don't want your girlfriends daydreaming about sleeping with your guy – or worse. Boasting or complaining about your active sex life may get you empathy or sympathy, but it may also trigger some between-the-sheets curiosity from your envious sounding board. We all know that curiosity killed the cat. Unfortunately, you won't have that as an option. So when it comes to sex with your significant other, hold on to this rule: Silence is golden.

> **"Boasting or complaining about your active sex life may get you empathy or sympathy, but it may also trigger some between-the-sheets curiosity from your envious sounding board. We all know that curiosity killed the cat. Unfortunately, you won't have that as an option."**

Drama Queens

If you have someone in your life who seems to have been born with a crazy gene, beware. It's only a matter of time before you too will be on the wrong end of his or her drama. "Crazy" friends are usually narcissistic, co-dependent energy vampires who will suck the life out of you and drop you when you no longer serve their purposes. It isn't easy to get out of bed with them once you're in, so avoid wasting time, and don't allow these toxic Drama Queens to creep into your life in the first place.

Gossipmongers

Do not forget that women (or men) who gossip to you will gossip about you. Just as they tell you the secrets of other friends, you can bet those friends hear your secrets too.

When it comes to gossipmongers, shield your heart and close your mouth. Gossipmongers may seem interesting and enchanting, but they're disloyal. Gossipmongers use information about you to endear themselves to other women in an act of false intimacy. They'll use your secrets (frequently adding their own embellishments if the truth is not tantalizing enough) to bait others into sharing their secrets.

Gossipmongering works like a twisted "pay it forward" scheme. If it's so juicy you must tell someone, the person in whom you confide is going to feel the same way and do the same thing. They will inevitably tell at least one other person, and that person will tell another, and like that old telephone game we played in school, on and on the story will continue to be told. If you don't want your secret to be told, don't tell it!

> **"Gossipmongers use information about you to endear themselves to other women in an act of false intimacy."**

Snakes

When you're warned that someone is a snake, believe it the first time. Don't kid yourself for one minute into thinking that you're such a snake charmer that you won't be bitten. Stay around long enough and you'll be bitten every time. It's the law of nature.

Dirty Laundry

The closer you are with people, the more likely you are to have disagreements with them. How you sort out these inevitable conflicts will determine the fate of your relationships.

I've seen close friendships severed because people chose to say nothing to a friend with whom they've had a problem and instead elected to air their "dirty laundry" in public. This further complicates the situation by bringing in a degree of public humiliation, which tends to escalate what should have been a heart-to-heart between friends into a public war of words. A private war fought publicly may inflict wounds so deep that a lifelong friendship becomes a friendship lost forever.

If you care about your friend, try to communicate swiftly, clearly and, most importantly, privately. Ask yourself if you'd rather be right or if you'd rather be happy. It's important to respect and nurture your friendships. If you do, your girlfriends will always be there for you, even if your husbands come and go!

Bee Stings

Don't mix all your friends together. It's better to have several sets. As cozy as the notion of a big, happy posse of friends may seem, women can be extremely catty and competitive. If one Queen Bee or a bunch of drones get angry with you, they have been known to congregate and go after you like a swarm of killer bees. It's easier to get stung by a few, isolated bees than to deal with the toxic reaction caused by the sting of your entire social circle.

Becoming More

It was the brilliantly talented Rita Wilson Hanks who first taught me about people "becoming more." Rita said when someone "becomes more" – as in more famous, more successful or more powerful – they also garner the confidence to become "more" of who they really are. "Becoming more" can be a good thing or a bad thing. One thing for sure, the revealing process is always interesting to watch.

One of my most amusing encounters of someone "becoming more" has to do with a very famous movie star (one degree of separation) who left the nicest telephone message asking if I would please return her call. She made a point of stating she was leaving me her home number so I could reach her directly.

When I returned the call, she didn't remember she'd called me. In fact, she rudely insisted that she didn't call at all. I reminded her that she actually did. She then shouted, "I didn't give you my home number!" I nicely reiterated that she specifically asked me to call her at her home, otherwise, I wouldn't have access to her private home number. She finally realized she must have called. Her next comment was "Well, I must have been calling you to decline something!" My jaw dropped, and I remember thinking, *Wow, she certainly became more – more of a %#$%@!*

It turned out this Oscar-nominated diva forgot she had called to ask me a favor. She wanted to see if the charity I'm involved with, Cedar's Sinai Medical Center C.O.A.C.H. For Kids (a member of the Children's Health Fund's national pediatric mobile medical program), could help a charity she worked with. I did the favor.

Pay attention to people "becoming more," and you'll learn a great deal about character. You'll also have your own amusing stories to tell. Hopefully, yours will be good stories of people "becoming more" wonderful!

Queen Bees

Queen Bees are women who have attained their queenly status by being pushy, powerful, ruthless, talented, beautiful, connected or rich. They're accustomed to their word being the last on most matters.

Every community has its fair share of Queen Bees who are able to maintain their status of being royally respected as long as they stay in the vicinity of their own hives. Problems always arise when a Queen Bee (or a Queen Wanna-Bee) attempts to expand her territory into another bee's nest. This can turn into a socially fatal mistake, as a Queen Bee will do whatever is necessary to protect her status.

It's important for all Queen Bees to understand that there's a hierarchy among Queen Bees and a host of silent rules that must be followed which allows each colony to buzz along in a civilized fashion. The most fundamental rule is that a Queen Bee should never buzz too quickly into another Queen's territory. I've seen many Queen Bees make the mistake of confidently buzzing into a new bee hive, only to be permanently exterminated by the reigning Queen and her drones.

Here are the basic rules you should know if you find yourself in the vicinity of a buzzing beehive:

Always be respectful of a Queen Bee's status, no matter how she got it.

Acting like a Queen Bee doesn't make you a Queen Bee.

Pick your battles, hold your tongue and don't underestimate the ability of a Queen Bee to turn you into a drone if you don't play by her rules.

There can be socially-deadly poison contained in a sting by a Queen Bee.

Shoot the Messenger

Before you pass on explosive information to a friend, ask yourself, *What good purpose is served by passing on this information?* If there is none, then don't do it. If you decide there is a good reason, you better get out your bulletproof vest because you're probably going to need it!

That's especially true if you intend to pass on information regarding the private lives and sexcapades of others, even if it's your best friend's husband who is having an affair. Before you jump the gun to share your knowledge of the affair, you better really know your friend and know for a fact that she would want to find out.

Also, remember that even your best assumptions may be wrong. She may not want to know, she may already know, or she may even be embarrassed and distance herself from you as a result of your knowledge. Just because you *think* she would want to know the truth doesn't mean she'll want to hear it from you. You'd be surprised how many people subscribe to the belief that what they don't know won't hurt them – or compel them to file for divorce.

> **WARNING! WARNING! WARNING!**
>
> **You'd be surprised how many people subscribe to the belief that what they don't know won't hurt them – or compel them to file for divorce.**

If you decide to pass on the explosive information, you could be considered the troublemaking cause of their breakup. This may be fine, until they get back together and they decide to shoot the troublemaking messenger. Then – BANG! Your friendship is dead and out you go! It happens all the time.

WARNING! WARNING! WARNING!

MONEY

Money Matters

I wish I could tell you money doesn't matter, but it does. It really, really does. Money won't make you happy, but a lack of money will certainly make you miserable. Having enough money to support yourself and those you love is one of those harsh realities that has a direct correlation to the happiness, stability, and well-being of your family. You cannot be happy if you cannot support your family. You have to keep this in mind when making decisions for your future: money matters.

So, how much is enough? This is a relative question that only you can answer. I know some happy "rich" people and plenty of miserable ones too. Competing in a race for money is pointless. No matter how much you have, there will always be someone out there with more and someone else around to point it out.

Whether you make thirty thousand a year, hundreds of thousands, millions, or even billions, you will be happier in the long run if you live within your means and don't base your self-worth on your net worth. Plenty of people are now learning this lesson the hard way, as the current economic downturn is cause for so many reversals of fortune. It's essential that you become extremely responsible with managing your money and investments in order to safeguard yourself from being Madoff'd. All the hope in the world is not going to change the fact that America is going to have some tough years ahead, and, in all likelihood, you will too.

It's never wise to ignore your financial situation. Read *Who Moved My Cheese?* by Spencer Johnson. Your ability to survive changing circumstances is determined by how prepared you are and how quickly you react. If there are storm clouds in the distance, then start seeking shelter now.

The Oprah Theory

You can be more successful than 99 percent of all the women in the world, and you still won't be able to afford an apartment on Fifth Avenue overlooking Central Park or a house in Beverly Hills north of Sunset. No matter how smart, capable, ambitious, or successful you think you can be, there is still only one Oprah Winfrey.

It continues to be a man's world in many ways. You need to know it, understand it, and find a way to make it for work for you. You can even try to change it, but don't kid yourself for one minute into believing that your equal rights will translate to equal opportunity without double the effort and sacrifice made by men.

Don't be surprised if you find that the doors of economic opportunity don't fling open to welcome you. You must be prepared to force the doors open. To do so, arm yourself with as much education as you can afford, get the best experience possible, and form strong alliances. Then, brace yourself with courage and do your best to burst through those doors and crash through the glass ceiling, even if you have to do it with a baby on your hip!

Remember, no matter how successful you are, you will always be happier if you measure the riches of your life by the gratitude in your heart. And never forget: Happiness is the byproduct of gratitude – in any economy.

There may indeed be only one Oprah Winfrey, but there is also only one you! So be your own best friend, dream big, aim high, make smart decisions, and work hard to control the destiny of your own fabulous life.

Shopping Therapy

Do you love shopping? Does the thrill of having something new make your heart pound? Do new shoes make you feel five pounds thinner? Does shopping provide you with a distraction from the worries of the world?

Many women like to think of shopping as therapy, but some of them are actually addicted to shopping, albeit this is fine if you are a wealthy woman. On the other hand, if you are like most women, you are not shopping to help out the economy but are instead impulsively shopping to the detriment of your financial stability.

How do you know if your shopping "therapy" is actually a dangerous addiction? It's simple. Just answer these questions. Do you carry a credit card balance? Do you ever feel guilty about shopping? Do you buy things you never wear? Do you hide purchases from your husband? Do you have at least eight months' savings put away? Do you have enough money for retirement?

If you are not spending 100 percent debt-free discretionary income (or if you don't know what that is), then now is not the time to be spending for sport. Cut back – way back. Start by using cash or your debit card, and no more impulse buying. Stop buying your children "five-minute" toys. Go through your closet and wear what you have. Don't be afraid of alterations. Think of reworking the clothes in your closet as a style challenge. (I hear thrift-store-vintage is the new black label.)

As a result of our economic challenges, many women have to cut back, be creative, and manage their money like never before. I highly recommend you read Suze Orman's book, *Women & Money* and Jean Chatzky's book, *Make Money, Not Excuses.* There is no excuse for squandering away money. Excuses are not going to pay your bills.

Patriotic Shopping

How can you justify sport shopping when so many people around you are suffering from the economic crisis? Here is how: If you have more money than you will ever need, then shopping is the very best thing you can personally do for the economy right now. In fact, shop until you drop. It keeps the money flowing.

Put the American flag bumper sticker on your Bentley, grab your Hermes bag, throw on your Prada jacket, head over to Neiman's, Saks, or Bergdorf's and take a little detour through Dolce & Gabbana, Louis Vuitton, Valentino, Yves St. Laurent, and Chanel. Then, pick up some sexy new lingerie at La Perla, and check into the Montage for a weekend rendezvous with your significant other.

In fact, why stop there? You don't have a Black American Express for nothing! Speed dial Net-Jet and take your children and your in-laws to Maui! Check into the lovely Grand Wailea where they can enjoy waterslide heaven. Then wheels up again. Fly to my favorite piece of paradise, Bora Bora, and hotel hop between the St. Regis, Le Meridien, The Four Seasons and Private Island Taha'a.

But let's bring this a bit more down to Earth. You don't need luxury brands and mountains of cash to stimulate the economy. Start in your own community by supporting and buying from local farmers. Buy the freshest foods at your farmer's market, and bring your family and friends together for a simple, pot-luck feast. Open a bottle of wine, and toast the incredible people you're blessed to have in your life.

Seriously, don't feel guilty for having money and spending it. Every penny you spend helps keep someone else employed. If you can afford to spend it, then spend it! Spend it for Uncle Sam! Consider it your patriotic duty!

Prenuptial Agreements

If your husband-to-be is of substantial means, he may surprise you by slipping a beautiful engagement ring on your left hand and simultaneously slapping a "prenuptial agreement" in your right. This unexpected presentation of a "prenup" always provides a highly-charged emotional challenge for any dreamy-eyed bride-to-be and frequently triggers her to look for the exit door instead of the altar.

Most young brides are years away from understanding the future implications of what they are negotiating. **Although most women don't realize it at the time, a husband-to-be is likely to be more generous when he is head-over-heels in love than he might be later down the line if he happens to fall out of love with you and decides to go on a lifetime retreat with his yoga instructor.**

Here are a couple things to remember. First, distance yourself from fighting over this agreement. Hire an experienced attorney to negotiate for you. Keep in mind, that you are entering into a partnership, and what you bring to the partnership is perhaps not economic power, but the equally important contribution of creating and raising a family. You are negotiating not only for yourself, but also for your future children. What you agree to now may later turn out to be what you and your children have to live with (or without) in the future. Most men don't become more generous after they decide to divorce, so do your best negotiating now.

Make sure that the economic terms of the post-marriage lifestyle agreement are acceptable in the event that you and your children are on your own. You don't want to devote the best years of your life to your marriage to then find yourself and your children financially disrespected and living in hardship while your ex-husband lives the high life with his new replacement wife and family. The bottom line? Never sell your soul – and don't give it away either.

Little Nest Eggs

A woman should always have a nest egg of her *own* money safely stashed away. **Psychologically, it is important to know that if you ever find yourself in a situation where you need to jump ship, you can at least pay for a lifeboat that will get you safely to shore.**

Any financially catastrophic situation could likely take you much longer to regroup than in years past. In case of an unpredictable emergency such as job loss, bankruptcy, divorce, personal injury or illness, death of spouse, etc., your goal should be to have enough savings put away to tide you over for *at least* eight months.

If your husband is the breadwinner and circumstances *necessitate* divorce, you still have to have your own money. You will have to pay a retainer fee for a divorce attorney. You should also be able to pay your bills and take care of your children's needs for at least several months in the event that your husband refuses to help you financially prior to the insistence of the judge.

It's amazing how the consistent income and dependable assets of so many husbands seem to mysteriously disappear with the filing of divorce papers. Men often use a woman's economic vulnerability for emotional leverage and financial manipulation.

You need to have your ducks in a row and be able to take care of the financial needs of your family before you take action that may harm them in the long run. (If you are in a dangerous or abusive situation, none of these rules apply. Just be smart, seek professional guidance and get yourself and your children to safety.) Having your own money can give you freedom to stay or freedom to go. **If you don't feel trapped, you may not feel the need to escape.**

Economic Crisis Syndrome

Economic Crisis Syndrome (ECS) is an anxiety-related condition that affects both men and women. ECS is triggered by the fear or possibility of total economic collapse. Sufferers of ECS exhibit a wide range of symptoms including anxiety, panic, fear, insomnia, heart palpitations, anger, resentment, short temper, depression, loss of sexual desire (especially for your spouse), infidelity and the impulse to call a divorce attorney.

It's no surprise that money problems are cited as the number one reason for divorce. Pay attention. If you see symptoms of ECS, you must determine if they are based on fear or actual circumstance. If your husband's ability to provide for your family is truly challenged, ECS may cause your respect and affection for him to wane. You may find yourself feeling trapped and looking for a way out – not just out of your money crisis, but also out of your marriage.

It's also not uncommon for extramarital affairs to coincide with a bout of ECS – making "Which came first, the infidelity or the money problems?" a difficult question for outsiders to answer. The truth is, many men find it easier to attribute their money problems to divorce rather than the emasculating fact that they're suffering severe financial problems. For men, divorce can be used to escape the burden of financial accountability that's expected in marriage. If you're noticing symptoms of ECS, you should immediately begin treatment with a combination of stress management, financial crisis management, marriage counseling, therapy, sex, and repetition of the Serenity Prayer. You have to be strong, supportive and smart. No matter how difficult the financial stress is on your marriage, you and your children are likely to fare much better if you manage to keep your marriage together.

For Richer and Poorer

If you're married and experiencing Economic Crisis Syndrome, stay calm and go into solution mode, not divorce mode. You and your spouse need to understand that this is a rough time for everyone (not just you), and it will be even tougher if you spend your time beating each other up. Destroying what's left of your husband's self-esteem is not going to do either one of you any good.

You have to figure out a plan to manage your way through these challenging times, and that may include making some serious lifestyle adjustments. Just the term "lifestyle adjustment" is enough to trigger ECS in many women, as we don't readily take to downsizing. Unfortunately, there may be no other choice.

You need to be strong for your husband, and you need to protect your children from emotional stress. They don't need to lie awake at night worrying about the dire situation in the world. And making their father feel like a total loser is definitely not in their best interest.

You should reassess your own ability to financially contribute to the household. This is no time to be proud, and you must do whatever you can to help the family. Exchange services and barter if you have to. Tough times require you to think outside of the box and be financially creative. Watch *The Big Idea with Donny Deutsch* on the internet (or just watch Donny Deutsch!) and get inspired. Come up with an idea of your own that can make you extra income. You and your husband need to make forward-thinking decisions that will keep your family ahead of the storm.

It's not difficult to convince men to leave when the going gets rough, so don't push your limits. You need your husband, and your children need their dad. Don't you hate the "for richer, for poorer" part of the deal?

Economic Depression

The economy has gone to hell in a handbasket. You may lose your home, your job, and/or your savings. You may have to move from your home. You may have to ask friends, relatives or the government for help. Loved ones may ask you for loans, jobs, food or shelter. It may all seem like too much to handle, but you cannot let "fear of the unknown" steal your life away.

No matter what your circumstances, this is no time for emotional collapse. If you are staring into the void, read Arianna Huffington's book, *On Becoming Fearless.* She says, "Fearlessness is not the absence of fear. Rather, it's the mastery of fear. It's getting to the point where our fears do not stop us from daring to think new thoughts, try new things, take risks, fail, and start again. Fearlessness is all about getting up one more time than we fall down." Right now, you have to get up.

If your faith has been jolted, try a weekly dose of televised inspiration from Joel Osteen, the best–selling author and senior pastor of the Lakewood Church in Houston, Texas. It doesn't matter what religion you are, Joel Osteen is a messenger of self-empowerment. His message will fuel your spirit and strengthen your belief – not just in yourself, but also in a higher power that will guide you through your darkest hours.

For less than the cost of a therapy session, you can get a yearly subscription to XM/Sirius Satellite Radio. You can listen to Oprah's Soul Series featuring enlightened teachers like Deepak Chopra, Eckart Tolle, Dr. Maya Angelou, Marianne Williamson, Dr. Robin Smith and Rabbi Shmuley.

If you can find a way to stay connected to your spirit, you will survive this economic crisis. Accepting the things you cannot change does not mean you give up hope. Have faith. The sun will shine again.

Hit Them in the Wallet

Are you tired of being at the mercy of the media? It's hard enough to keep marriages on track without the bombardment of advertising encouraging men to have affairs. Enough is enough! Women make up half of this country, and we have two things going for us that can make us highly effective if we decide to unite and go toe-to-toe with the media. First of all, we control the purchasing power in our homes. Secondly, we have massive email lists of like-minded friends who are only one send-button away.

Let's take the example of a theoretical in-your-face billboard that says something offensive like, "Forget your wife – cheat tonight." (As if men need any more encouragement.) The goal is to get the advertisement taken down in your neighborhood. Boycotting that Internet company would be meaningless. So in a case like this, a boycott can still be effective if it's targeted to the other woman-centric companies who advertise with the same billboard company.

First, find the biggest female-targeted consumer product advertisers doing business with the billboard company and hit them in the wallet with a boycott. Tell them why and ask for their help to assist you by using their considerable media buying power to "encourage" the outdoor media company to remove the offensive billboards.

When they remove the billboard, your giant posse of women with computers will call off the boycott and celebrate by buying lots of the big company's products, and everyone is happy. It only takes a few effective boycotts for companies to get the powerful message *Warrior Wives* can send with our wallets. See, we have learned a thing or two from men. Never underestimate the effectiveness of a great community organizer!

Life's Little Trade-Offs

You know the story: She's beautiful, and he is rich, and the derogatory word "gold digger" often jumps out of the mouths of men (and some women) taking note of the situation. For some reason, men have a gender bias that keeps them from understanding the true dynamics in this conspicuous union of "Beauty And The Beast."

Yes, it's true that she probably woudn't have married him if standing on his wallet didn't make him look six inches taller in her eyes, but does that make her a gold digger? **Here is the question that should be posed to the oh-so-judgmental men and women: Would "The Wallet" be with the "Gold Digger" if she was the exact same woman with the same beautiful face and charming personality, but carried an extra fifty pounds around the middle?** Their answer is, of course, a resounding "No!"

This awe-inspiring pairing doesn't make a woman a gold digger, and it doesn't make the man a shallow creep. They probably wouldn't be together (or more accurately, *stay* together) if it weren't for love. Throughout history, the mating game has always been based on the same principle, "survival of the fittest," and this is just another flamboyant example.

Beautiful women have an advantage in attracting a well-providing caveman, and the well-providing caveman gets to show off his superior hunting ability by flaunting the beautiful woman he gets to share his cave with. You can't fight Mother Nature.

There are exceptions, of course, and real gold diggers (versus women who just look like gold diggers) are out there. But you can trust that men who marry these women know exactly who they're exchanging vows with. You can be sure that one way or another, they're each getting exactly what they want. Think of it as just another one of life's little trade-offs.

Financing Your Golden Years

Imagine what your life will be like when you're sixty-five. Will you be shopping for a new Chanel bag or pushing a shopping cart full of Hefty bags? No woman ever dreams that one day she may be poor, old and living in the streets – but it does happen, and you better believe it.

Every woman, married or not, should plan ahead and prepare for her golden years. A woman's longevity is her blessing, and sometimes even her curse. Unfortunately, our longer lifespan also increases the risk we will outlast our savings accounts.

Let's begin with the facts. The average woman will live to be over eighty years old! That's a lot of retirement years to finance. If you're married, you'll probably outlive your husband by seven years. If he's older, you may outlive him by ten, twenty, or even thirty years. Did you know the average age of an American widow is fifty-five?

To avoid outliving your savings, you have to plan ahead. Live within your means. Pay off your credit cards and maintain strict discipline about saving money for retirement. If you're married, make sure your husband maintains his life insurance policy with you as the beneficiary. And goodness gracious, if you are married, don't blindly trust your husband when he "says" he's got it covered. Make sure that he really has it covered.

In order to safeguard your future, you need to make it your business to know every detail about your finances, or else you could be the one left holding the bag, and it probably won't be Chanel. Just remember when you see a woman living on the streets pushing a cart, she never thought for a moment that she would be in that sad situation. So give her some money, say a prayer, skip the cappuccino, and go make a deposit into your savings account!

Mindful Spending

What do you waste your money on? Try to figure out how much you can save by being mindful with your spending. Grab a pencil and a calculator. Write a list of everything you waste money on for one month. Below are some categories to help you get started. Then, start totaling up the amount of money you are spending on guilty pleasures that you can learn to live without.

Coffee/soda/drinks:
Impulse grocery shopping:
Junk food:
Alcohol:
Cigarettes:
Bottled water:
Beauty products and services:
Dining out:
Interest charges:
Unused memberships:
Media and magazines:
Premium gas and travel:
Clothes and shoes:
Five Minute toys:
Household expenses:
Technology:
Entertainment:
Other:
Total savings for a month ______________________=
Total savings for the year ______________________=
Total savings for 10 years ______________________=
Just a little something to think about!

WARNING! WARNING! WARNING!

DATING

A Few Decisions

There are a few important decisions that every woman makes somewhere between her late-teens and mid-twenties that will dictate the course of the rest of her life.

If you are in your early twenties, then I suggest you pause from your busy social life and wrap your head around the importance of this concept. If you're already looking over your shoulder on these years, then you know exactly what those few decisions were (both the good and bad ones) that got you where you are right now.

If you are a young woman, it's a great advantage for you to be fully aware of how significant these early decisions are. Here are a few of those fate-determining choices that will play a huge part in setting the path for your future: Will you stay in your hometown or move to another city? Will you get a college degree or drop out of school? Will you have a profession or move from job to job? Will you marry the right guy or the wrong guy, or will you get married at all? Will you get involved with drugs or alcohol? Will you fall in love with someone who is struggling with addiction? Will you make a sex video that ends up on the Internet? Will you manage your money or squander it away? Will you marry a successful man or a man who can't hold a job? Will you have a child out of wedlock? Will you stay married or get divorced? Will you have children early or wait too long?

If you are a young woman, ready or not, you are soon going to make some of the most critical and far-reaching decisions of your life. So wake up! Be smart. Don't let luck determine your destiny. Start mindfully creating the life of your dreams or risk having your future turn into your worst nightmare.

A House Is Not a Home

It's not the size of the house that will make you happy but the love in the home. If you are happy in a little house, you will be happy in a big house. This is not always the case vice versa.

It's Easy to Fall in Love

They say it's just as easy to fall in love with a rich man as it is with a poor man. This is true only if you don't date poor men! Always remember this: It is a woman's nature to nurture. Women can fall in love with anyone whose company we keep or in whose bed we sleep.

> **"Sex has a way of disconnecting the brains from the hearts of even the most intelligent women."**

A woman has to be careful about spending time between the sheets with the kind of man she doesn't want to marry. Sex has a way of disconnecting the brains from the hearts of even the most intelligent women. **If you don't want to marry a bartender, then don't sleep with bartenders!** If you don't want to marry an alcoholic, a drug addict, a con man, a struggling actor or a traveling salesman, then don't sleep with one in the first place.

The magical power of what happens between the sheets can brainwash even the smartest women into making decisions that can ruin their lives.

> There is a place you can touch a woman that will drive her crazy. Her heart.
>
> —MELANIE GRIFFITH

The Amazing Race

In the book *The Woman Who Never Evolved*, anthropologist Sarah Blaffer Hrdy says competition among females is a major determinant in primate social organization. Hrdy claims that from a Darwinian perspective, what drives primates (including humans) to compete is their intrinsic desire to ensure the well-being and survival of their offspring.

She was initially baffled when a study *seemed* to contradict her observations on the "genetic drive to compete" and found that highly educated women who were successful in their careers, stopped competing in the corporate world after having children.

Although this seems to be counterintuitive, these women actually were competing at the highest level of the evolutionary stratosphere. Apparently, these successful women instinctively knew that the best thing they could do to ensure the well-being of their children was to raise them themselves. So they married a suitable, highly educated husband who took care of the finances and they took care of the children. They even had a backup plan: If the marriage didn't work out, they would return to their established careers. This "master plan" was their insurance policy for the success of their little darlings.

There is no finer example than First Lady, Michelle Obama. She has made it explicitly clear that her number one priority is to raise her children well. **You can bet that the Obama girls are not going to flunk out of school, eat themselves into obesity, post naked pictures on the Internet, or have a baby before they get their driver's licenses.** No, not a chance! You want to know why? Because "Michelle O-Mama" is in the White House doing her job! Smart women do not rely on luck to determine the fate of their family. Smart women make smart decisions – and they see to it that their children follow in their highly educated footsteps.

One Princess in the House Theory

If your main attraction to a guy is his great looks or your big worry is his not-so-great looks, just remember that in both cases, the advice is the same. **There should only be one princess in the house, and it should be you.**

The Princess and the Truck Driver Theory

If you're a "princess" and your significant other is a "truck driver," you probably think, "Oh, surely he won't cheat on me because he's already scored with a babe who is clearly out of his league, right?" Wrong! Men who earn less that their wives, cheat even more. Just think Eva Longoria, Christie Brinkley, Diane Lane and Reese Witherspoon. These are the women who other men dream of, and yet even these guys still went out for junk food when they had filet mignon at home.

If you have a better job, more money, more fame, more fortune, more education, or more of just about anything, there is reason enough for him to feel like less of a man. **When a man doesn't feel "man enough," he will often seek the affection of other women who, at least for a few brief moments, make him feel like a king.**

The fragile egos of men often compel them to cheat when they don't feel worthy of the woman they have in their life.

Gravitation can not be held responsible for people falling in love.

—ALBERT EINSTEIN

The Uncivilized Man

Treat her like a lady? Not anymore! Treat her like a hooker is more like it! **It's a tough world out there for single women when the majority of men are so jaded that they no longer offer to pay for dinner, they rarely offer to buy a drink, and if they hear the word "no" from a woman, they just say, "Next!"**

Women today have some serious challenges when it comes to finding a partner for life. It's hard for a nice woman to compete for the attention of an Internet generation of cybersex addicted men who expect women to drop their clothes the moment they meet and *perform* like women who are accustomed to having sex with the camera rolling.

You have to wonder, in the age of porn, is romance dead? The instant gratification of Internet porn has contributed to men becoming desensitized to love and romance. Today's generation of men are disproportionately over-sexed, hyper-stimulated and continually chasing an instant sexual thrill the way a drug addict chases the first high. Modern men operate with a "live and let live" philosophy that says to heck with family, wives, children, responsibility and accountability. This new generation of men has little regard for self-sacrifice or putting the values of family in front of the satisfaction of immediate gratification. It's no wonder more women are single than married in America!

Women are being forced to raise their children alone while the fathers of their children are out with a revolving door of young women – who think nothing of having sex with a man who won't even buy them breakfast in the morning. Who is to blame? The men, the women, or the times we live in?

How in the world are you supposed to find a great husband when you can't find great men to start with? I don't want to scare you, but if you're single, the truth is you're going to have to look harder than ever to find Prince Charming (or even a frog with royal potential). There are still plenty of men of integrity available, but they're unlikely to be found in obvious places. These men are going about their business, living lives that are undramatic and completely unworthy of a reality show. These men are also hoping to find the rare woman of substance who doesn't drop her panties with the flash of a credit card or treat sex like she's a porn star on an audition.

By the way, if you don't have strong marriage and family values or live your life with integrity, you can forget about attracting a guy who does. If you find yourself dating a narcissistict male who says he's not looking for a commitment, believe him! You can be assured he's not into you – at least not beyond physically. He's not even into you enough to fake being into you. Don't fool yourself into thinking he's going to change and one day shower you with roses. You'll be lucky to get a rose on Facebook from these thrill-seeking cybersex-addicted playboys. And even if you do, he probably emailed the same rose to ten other women that same afternoon!

> **"It's a tough world out there for single women when the majority of men are so jaded they no longer offer to pay for dinner, they rarely offer to buy a drink, and if they hear the word "no" from a woman they just say next."**

Keep your personal standards high and keep looking in unexpected places for those fabulous men who value qualities in women that aren't sold on the Internet or exchanged for a weekend in a luxury hotel. **If you sell your soul when you're young, you'll pay the price when you're old.**

The Shop Girl

Smart, attractive, hard-working, professional women often shake their heads and wonder how it happened; that the women they used to think of as uneducated "shop girls" are now the ones married to successful guys, raising families, and living in beautiful homes. How did this happen?

Here's how: The shop girl never thought for a moment that she was going to be Oprah Winfrey. She knew having the good life wasn't going to happen because of her ambition, intelligence, talent or breathtaking beauty. She knew that her youth and sex-appeal were diminishing assets, and she didn't squander hers away. She made time to date regular guys, and married a nice hardworking man who climbed the ladder of success with her by his side.

The "smart girl," on the other hand, spent her "beautiful years" being arrogant and overly focused on her career. She thought she was so fabulous that time wouldn't be a factor for her and that the "perfect man" would just show up when the time was right. Wrong!

First and foremost, it took the smart girl far too long to realize there's no such thing as a "perfect man" – that's just an urban legend. Secondly, in hindsight she found the men who weren't good enough before are miraculously looking pretty perfect – now that her clock has ticked past midnight. Unfortunately these men are no longer available or are no longer interested in some aging beauty who is *trying* to look young, no matter how smart she is.

Many smart women don't realize how desirable youth is to a man until they no longer have their youth, which is coincidentally how long it takes them to realize there's no such thing as the perfect man. This is the mistake smart women refer to when they look enviously at the life of the happy shop girl and whisper to their friend, "I was just a little too smart."

The Psychologist Theory

Remember that a wonderful guy who talks to you, understands you, pays attention to everything you say, and is totally sensitive to your needs is usually a guy who can't make a living. That's what girlfriends are for!

Potential

If you're going to marry "potential" as in, "He's a writer and doesn't have a car right now, but it looks like he's going to sell a screenplay…" then you better really, really love him and be equally prepared to love him "for richer or poorer" if his screenplay doesn't pan out.

If the only happy reality with your guy depends on his "potential," you'd better think twice before considering marriage. Having faith in potential is one thing if you are twenty-something, however, if you are over thirty, choosing to be involved with a man who has potential in the future, but nothing going on in the present can be a big mistake.

> **One of the greatest factors in divorce is an unrealistic financial expectation.**

One of the greatest factors in divorce is an unrealistic financial expectation. If you expect your husband to be the primary breadwinner in the family, then you'd better be happy with the bread he bakes every day. If you wait years and years hoping for the perfect loaf to rise and it never does, you'll resent the loaf you married.

Over Forty, Every Year Is a Dog Year

If you want to get married, you don't want to be forty and single, no matter how great you are. You don't want to be thirty-five and single either. I don't even want to talk about forty-five!

No matter how fabulous you are, if getting married and having children are priorities to you, then don't wait until you are forty to get serious about it. This especially holds true if you want to be a first wife and have the first (and hopefully only) family. In fact, if you're cruising anywhere near thirty-five, you don't want to waste another minute. Step it up quickly with your dating. Call in your posse of friends and ask them to do some recruiting for you. Take some pointers from Patti Stanger, and watch *Millionaire Matchmaker*. This is the time you need to put your best self forward and fill up your dance card while the faint tick of your biological clock is still loud enough for some men to hear.

> **Age comes upon us gradually in our twenties and thirties. After the age of forty, women age as if every year is a dog year!**

Age comes upon us gradually in our twenties and thirties. After the age of forty, women age as if every year is a dog year!

> Forty is the old age of youth; fifty is the youth of old age.
>
> —VICTOR HUGO

Not Young, Not Married, Not Happy

If you're reading this book and thinking – *Oh my gosh! I'm not young, not beautiful, and not married! I'm going to shoot myself* – don't! There really is someone for everyone, including you, if that's what you want.

Remember your last trip to Disney World? You saw fat people, old people, young people, people in wheelchairs, people on crutches, people who are blind, and people who are deaf. Every kind of person you can imagine is strolling down Main Street holding hands with someone they love. Do they all have so much more going for them than you? No. So what's the difference? They, one way or another, got to know someone and fell in love. They didn't sit around the office or their home waiting for the perfect man to climb down the chimney with a wedding ring. They went out and found him – or made themselves findable for him.

If you really want to be married, then stop your dreaming and wishful thinking. Snap out of it! Get busy! Stop wasting time thinking it's just "going to happen," because it may not if you don't put your energy into *making* it happen.

If your looks don't stop traffic, then stop walking the streets! Forget about wasting time trying to attract the eye of a drive-by window shopper. Seek situations where a guy can get to know you, not just see you. It's all about access! Never lose sight of this fact: There are still just as many fish in the sea as there are caught in other women's nets, so stop strolling up and down the beach! Go get yourself a pole and find a well-stocked fishin' hole!

The Frog Masquerade

When women tell stories of the men they could have married, they often cite the same mistake: They regrettably dismissed the real princes for being frogs. When they look back on their mistakes, they realize they were foolishly arrogant and turned down great guys for all kinds of superficial reasons like physical characteristics such as being too short, too fat, too bald, too boring or too hairy. Sometimes, the reasons were as simple as not liking his shoes, his car, the color of his house, or the way he danced – a plethora of stupid and regrettable reasons.

Then, one by one, these "oh-so-fabulous" women watched themselves get older, and these so-called *frogs* got married and created fabulous lives with their grateful wives.

"The real princes are often out there masquerading as frogs, just waiting for the right girl to recognize them in their disguise."

The real princes are often out there masquerading as frogs, just waiting for the right girl to recognize them in their disguise. Of course, there are just as many frogs masquerading as princes, but that's a different lesson.

Be smart. Accept this fact: There are no perfect men.

Learn to distinguish between a frog and a prince. Otherwise, you too could become another aging beauty, once too good for all but the most perfect men, now looking for a prince on the Internet – not that there's anything wrong with that!

Dating Married Men

Stay away from married men! If there's any sure way to sell your soul, sleeping with a married man is it. It will ruin your reputation, erode your self-respect and steal your life away. He'll lie to be with you, and he'll lie to you.

Married men frequently lure women into their life of deception by doing things like removing their wedding ring and pretending they are not married. He may tell you (lie) he is separated but still living in the same house – because of the children. He may tell you (lie) his wife is like his sister and they are sleeping in separate rooms. He may tell you (lie) he will divorce when the children get out of the house. He may give you money for rent and tell you (lie) he can't leave for business purposes so just hang in there with him. The cheating married man always has an excuse to buy time (sex) with a woman he is interested in – that is until *he* is tired of her.

If you've found your way into this dishonest, gut-wrenching nightmare, then you need to dig deep, down to the bottom of your long-forgotten soul and resurrect your dignity. Don't spare the horses getting away from him. (And FYI, it will be best for you if you do it before his wife reads this book.) If a man is getting a divorce, you should never be part of the reason. Cheating men seldom marry the woman they were cheating with when their wife found out. **Once their wives kick them out and they are free to date anyone they please, they no longer have to settle for a woman with so little character that she accepts crumbs from someone else's cheating husband.**

If the long shot happens and you do find yourself married to him, do not kid yourself. It is a fact: One day he absolutely will cheat on you too.

Bad Boy Addiction

You can kid yourself and call them "bad boys" if you like. However, "bad boys" are really "bad men," and they aren't likely to change. These men will ruin your life.

With these guys, your future is a miserable one. It will always be the same: drama after drama, making up and breaking up, insecurity and instability. If you're choosing these guys over and over, then you're choosing self-destruction. They don't destroy you; you destroy yourself by allowing them into your life.

If you're one of those women who jokes with a wink and a smile about your attraction and weakness for "bad boys," then I have news for you – your act is not as cute as you think. There is nothing funny about this destructive behavior. If you continue getting involved with bad boys, the word "bad" is going to apply to you as much as it does to them.

The heartache of bad boy addiction will slowly steal your life away. Get out while you can! Stay away from them if you want to save your future. If you can't do it on your own, then use the AA Twelve-Step Program and get your codependent, bad boy addiction under control. Your future is at stake.

Just Say No

You will never regret the "no's" you say in life. No to sex, no to drugs, no to just one more drink – no to just about anything. It's the "yes" that gets you in trouble. Whenever you have even a shred of doubt, just say no.

Holiday Hedging

Holidays, particularly Christmas, New Year's and Valentine's Day, are very important indicators of how your guy really feels about you. If you find your guy is hedging and not making specific holiday plans with you, or if he suddenly goes missing in action or takes a suspicious business trip on Valentine's Day, you've just found out what you need to know. In the infamous words of Greg Behrendt and Liz Tuccillo, "He's just not that into you."

If "your" guy doesn't want to spend the holidays with you, it's because he's up to monkey business! He's most likely spending it with another woman, perhaps even his wife! Another common reason for Holiday Hedging is so that he doesn't have to spend money giving you (and perhaps a chain of other women) a gift. He may also go MIA so he doesn't have to deal with the pressure of stepping up your "relationship" by introducing you to his friends or family.

Understanding the meaning of Holiday Hedging is very simple: If your guy is not with you during the holidays, then he's not in love with you. This may sound brutal, but it's true. It's always better to find out what you really need to know sooner rather than later. Time is too precious to waste on a man who is hedging.

Flings

The word "fling" sounds like so much fun (and they can be), but there are a few things you should keep in mind before you start dropping your clothes with some smooth-talking, studly wonder.

First of all, there are no secrets in the world. He'll definitely share news of his good score with someone, which means you'd better be sure that you don't mind being thought of as someone's score instead of someone's girlfriend or wife.

> **It's a small world, after all, so you better be sure a fling with "Mr. Right-Enough-Tonight" won't humiliate you tomorrow.**

Also, keep in mind that one can only have so many flings before others assign a less-than-charming label to you. It's a small world, after all, so you better be sure a fling with "Mr. Right-Enough-Tonight" won't humiliate you tomorrow.

> A reputation once broken may possibly be repaired, but the world will always keep their eyes on the spot where the crack was.
>
> —JOSEPH HALL

Sex with the Ex

Don't get in the habit of sleeping with your ex. It may seem like a harmless way to fulfill certain desires, but the truth is, it's far from emotionally safe. If you're sleeping with an ex, one of you (most likely you) will confuse the involvement, which will lead right back to the emotional drama of breaking up with someone you've already broken up with.

The bigger problem with sleeping with your ex is that when he fulfills your physical desires, you will find that days, weeks, and months can slip by, causing you to lose the urgency to find someone else worthy of sharing your *whole* life with. Sleeping with your ex is actually a harmful waste of your time, youth and beauty – and you know how I feel about that!

> **"The bigger problem with sleeping with your ex is that when he fulfills your physical desires, you will find that days, weeks, and months can slip by, causing you to lose the urgency to find someone else worthy of sharing your *whole* life with."**

When one door closes, another opens, but you will never find out as long as you continue using your panties as a door wedge.

The Rejection Hotline

The dating world is brutal – so brutal, in fact, that both men and women have found resourceful new ways of sending a clear message to nightclub stalkers who can't seem to take "no" for an answer. They don't just scribble a fake number on a Cosmo-stained cocktail napkin anymore. Instead, they scribble a city-specific fake number from RejectionHotline.com that, when called, will play the message they wish they had the courage to say.

When the number is dialed, a cheerful voice says something like, "You've reached the Rejection Hotline . . . unfortunately, the person who gave you this number did not want you to have their real number . . . " Then the voice rattles off a humorous host of possible reasons for the rejection – bad breath, body odor, or giving off that creepy psycho-stalker vibe. It continues with, "Please do your best to forget about the person who gave you this number because – trust us – they've already forgotten about you!" How is that for loud and clear?

> **"You'll get a message that'll bring you to your scuffed-up knees and make you think twice about hopping between the sheets with a handsome stranger the next time."**

A rejection message is sometimes not the only message that needs to be passed on. There are also numbers for messages that are situation-specific such as a Bad Breath Notification Number, a Body Odor Notification, a Booger Hanging Notification, and a One Night Stand Hotline.

By the way, if you get a Bad Breath Notification Number on your call log, guess what – people aren't just being mean. Chances are you have bad breath – REALLY bad breath! If anyone ever offers you a mint, don't ever say, "No, thanks." Just get the hint – and take the mint.

In the case of a one night stand, "Mr. I Thought You Were The Man Of My Dreams" may sweetly pass you the number to his "direct line" right alongside coffee and a bagel in the morning. He may then kiss your forehead, give you a George Clooney grin, and with a twinkle in his eye, say "call me" as he races out of the hotel room to catch his flight out of Vegas – so he can scurry back home to his wife and kids! When you call him and get the One Night Stand Hotline, you'll get a message all right! You'll get a message that'll bring you to your scuffed-up knees and make you think twice about hopping between the sheets with a handsome stranger the next time.

> **"You need to figure out what signal you are energetically sending out that makes creepy men think that with a little persistence you may say "yes.""**

If you end up getting one of these messages, then take heed. If you are repeatedly being dumped or duped by men, then I highly recommend you read Steve Harvey's book, *Act Like a Lady, Think Like a Man,* because no one should have to resort to giving that kind of message to you. If you're the one passing out a rejection hotline number, you need to stop wasting your time in nightclubs. You need to figure out what signal you are energetically sending out that makes creepy men think that with a little persistence you may say "yes." **If you act like a lady and look like a lady, you are more likely to be treated like a lady.** Think about that the next time you go out with your whale tail showing and your breasts playing peek-a-boo with any man over five feet tall.

The Glass Slipper Theory

I'm sorry to say that if it takes force to make the slipper fit, then you're not Cinderella, honey, and he's not your prince. When you're with the right guy, it feels right and it works – easily.

Getting along with each other shouldn't be difficult, especially in the beginning of a relationship. If getting along with your prince is a royal pain right out of the gate, you should see it as a big red flag warning you about the condition of the rough road that lies ahead.

As much as you may want to be Cinderella, you can't stretch a glass slipper. If the slipper doesn't easily fit, you will find that trying to walk in them on the rocky road of life only gets increasingly difficult as the years go by. Somewhere along the way, the slipper is bound to break, leaving you a heartbroken, aging princess in rags once again.

Bad Dog Journal

Pain has a short memory. When you break up with a guy, write down your reasons – all of them. Read them and re-read them, and if you ever consider going back to him (or someone like him), read them again and reconsider. If you do happen to get back together, odds are the next time you break up will be for the exact same reasons as before, and you'll have wasted even more of your precious time.

Keeping a Bad Dog Journal of a man's behavior (and misbehavior) is the best way to remember what you shouldn't forget.

Unmarried and Unlikely to Change

Some women are programmed for marriage, and some aren't. If you don't want be married or have children, then stop worrying about the expectations of your friends and family pressing you to waltz down the aisle. Go enjoy your freedom!

Marriage is not for everyone, and judging by the statistics, it certainly isn't the end-all for most women. When it goes wrong (which it does half the time), women are often left so vulnerable they wonder why they sacrificed so much of themselves to have it in the first place. **If you like being single and having total control of your life, finances and destiny, then maybe you need to get over thinking that "till death do us part" is right for you.** Maybe you're someone who needs to enjoy the modern world of being single and independent. And there's absolutely nothing wrong with that.

It works for Oprah; she calls the shots. She does what she wants, spends what she wants, and vacations wherever and whenever she wants. She has plenty of friends, and she looks terrific. I don't like to speculate about other people's sex lives, but Oprah has a twinkle in her eye that tells me she probably gets what she wants, the way she wants it, in that area too.

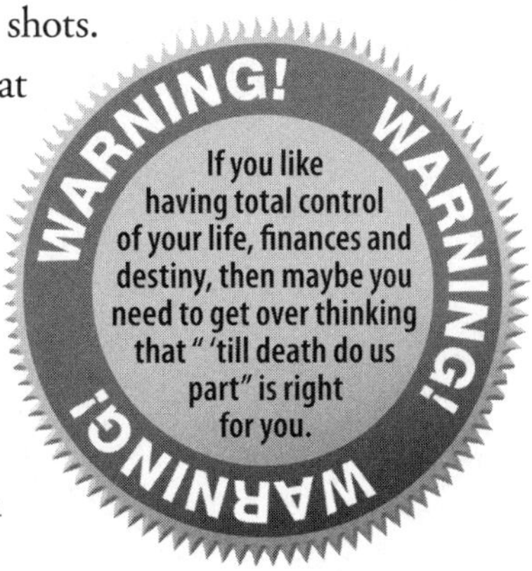

So if you're single, financially-independent, happy with your life and not longing for children, then stop worrying about having what you're not sure you want anyway. Go find your own Steadman and take one for the home team!

Divorced Men

Don't fear getting involved with a recently divorced man. They usually don't stay that way for long! As simple as it sounds, men who like to be married – like to be married. They aren't accustomed to being alone, so they typically don't get much time on the open market. In fact, divorced men usually remarry within three years of being divorced.

> **As simple as it sounds, men who like to be married – like to be married.**

However, beware of guys who are "repeat offenders" with multiple divorces. If this is the case for one of your prospects, you should make it your business to find out why and carefully analyze the reasons. If his marriages all ended because he cheated, his next marriage probably will too. The best predictor of a man's future behavior is his past behavior.

The Gift that Keeps on Giving

If you're going to have grown-up sex, then you better be ready to take on grown-up responsibility. If you impulsively decide to go to town with "Mr. Right-Enough-Tonight" and don't use a condom, he may hit it like a rock star, but don't assume you'll have a happy ending.

"Mr. Right-Enough-Tonight" may turn out to be one of the most unforgettable men of your life – particularly if he gives you the gift that keeps on giving: a pregnancy or a lifelong STD!

Love Shack

Don't live with a man unless you plan on marrying him. It really is as simple as that. Serial monogamists waste so much time shacking up with Mr. Not-Right-Enough-To-Marry, they don't register how quickly the years fly by.

Love-nesting ladies usually snap out of their Kurt Russell/ Goldie Hawn stupor when their relationship ends and they realize they've wasted the best years of their life "practicing" to be a wife when they could have actually been a wife. Living together gives you all the duties with none of the benefits of being married. Statistically, couples who live together before marriage are more likely to be divorced. Listen to Beyonce and stay a single lady unless he puts a ring on it. If you're going to live with him, marry him!

Mother Knows Best

If you're doing things you aren't proud to tell your mother about, you probably shouldn't be doing them. Let the mental approval of your mother guide your actions if your moral compass has gone so askew that your heart and mind are no longer connected to your body or your conscience.

Fast Forward

When dating, mentally project yourself ten years into the future, and ask yourself these important questions:

What does your life look like?

Where do you live?

How are you treated?

Where do your children go to school?

Where do you vacation?

How do you travel?

Do you work?

What does your husband do?

How do you look?

Who are your friends?

What brings you joy?

Now ask yourself, are you on the road to achieving the life you envision? Do the friends around you and the men you date match up with the future you desire? If you stay on the present road, will you get to where you want to be? I can't stress this enough: If you know where you want to be in the future, make sure the road you're on is one that will lead you there. In the words of Anthony Robbins, "If you do what you've always done, you'll get what you've always gotten."

A goal without a plan is just a wish.

—LARRY ELDER

Sizing Up A Date

If you allow your hands to "wander south" on the first date with a man you really like, only to discover a surprise package that would fit in your tampon holder, then you have a big, I mean a *little* border-crossing decision to make.

If you decide to act like an old-fashioned girl and retreat from this exploratory mission by not going any further on the first date, you may have accidentally reached the end of your exploration. He probably hasn't met an old-fashioned girl since high school and will likely think the reason you turned back was because you were turned off when you found a shortage on your hands – and perhaps you were.

The lesson here: Don't cross the Mason-Dixon Line with a guy you really like until you are ready to whistle "Dixie" and go to town!

However, if you really are an old-fashioned girl who thought he was fabulous and just didn't want him to think you were easy, your curiosity may have ruined what could have been a great thing. Unfortunately, it doesn't matter what excuse you make because he isn't going to believe you. And there's a good probability (even if you really like him) that he's never going to ask you out again. **Men hate feeling like their manhood has been sized up and dismissed, and they often transfer that negative feeling towards you.**

When it comes to *little* men with *big* egos, it's far easier for them to reject you than to ask to see you again and take a chance at being further rejected. The lesson here: Don't cross the Mason-Dixon Line with a guy you really like until you are ready to whistle "Dixie" and go to town!

Boring Men

One of the most common excuses I hear for a woman not being interested in a guy is that she finds him boring. What a mistake! **Dismissing a "boring guy" right out of the gate is often a decision that's regretted many years in the future when a woman looks back at her life and realizes that she passed over a series of wonderful "boring" guys only to endure years of heartache with a string of exciting, unpredictable men whose handsome faces could be immortalized in the Bi-Polar Hall of Fame.**

I encourage you to think twice before you dismiss the boring, consistent, predictable, hardworking, nice guys. These guys are often the ones you can count on when the going gets rough. They are much less likely to see rough water as an opportunity to jump ship and bail out for smooth sailing with someone else.

> **They say "Nice guys finish last." That's because they're the ones who will still be standing beside you when everyone else has come and gone!**

Think of boring men as a blank canvas of opportunity to create the life of your dreams. You can be the one to kick things up a notch. Just do some dog training! Spiff him up and give him a *GQ* makeover if the wrapping on the package is so important to you. And by the way, don't assume the boring guy doesn't have what it takes to rock your world when the lights go out!

They say "Nice guys finish last." That's because they're the ones who will still be standing beside you when everyone else has come and gone!

Older Men

Older men can be great husbands for some women. The upside is that you'll always be young compared to him, and he'll be less likely to leave when you turn fifty if he's already well over his mid-life crisis.

Also, older husbands tend to take marriage very seriously, as most men don't want to start over during their retirement years. An older man will appreciate your youth and beauty, and if his hard-working years paid off, he may now be in a place to slow down and fully appreciate his new family.

"Yes, it's true that no matter how old men are or what state of health they're in, they still want to have it going on down south, whether the equipment works or not."

Some of the happiest couples I know are couples with substantial age gaps between them. There is a lot to be said about men who proudly got it right on the "back nine." The downside is you may have very different energy levels when he hits his mid-sixties. In later years when his health starts to decline, you may be forced to slow down your energetic lifestyle in order to take care of his medical needs.

The real challenge in the twilight years of a May-December marriage comes at sundown when he expects you to shift positions from daytime nursemaid to nighttime sex goddess! Yes, it's true that no matter how old men are or what state of health they're in, they still want to have it going on down south, whether the equipment works or not. Now, doesn't that sound like fun!

Dog Training

Look, ladies, if he was *that* perfect when you found him, he probably wouldn't have been available. Sometimes you need to find a lovable mutt with an eager-to-please glint of potential in his eye and train him. That adventure can be a fun and worthwhile thing in and of itself.

You can't change the kind of dog he is, but you can clean and groom him and teach him a few of the more important house rules. If he's a liar, cheat, addict, or has a personality disorder, then forget it, because you just can't change things like that.

"Practicing this training program consistently can turn your loyal mutt into a champion show dog. Although personally, I think having a loyal mutt that looks nothing like a show dog may be the better way to go!"

If your big complaint is that he's socially awkward, dresses like a geek, has a house decorated like a college dorm, leaves the toilet seat up, or eats every meal like it's his last supper, you're in luck. These things can be changed.

Think of adjusting these basic behaviors as "dog training." The fundamental concept is simple: correction followed by treats, love and an abundance of praise. Practicing this training program consistently can turn your loyal mutt into a champion show dog. Although personally, I think having a loyal mutt that looks nothing like a show dog may be the better way to go!

So You Want to Be in Pictures

So your man thinks you look beautiful naked and wants to capture your beauty in a photograph? Just remember a beautiful picture is one thing, but a picture showing your "neenie" and your perky "chi-chi's" is quite another.

Think about what happened to the private tapes of Kim Kardashian and Paris Hilton, and remember you're playing with fire when it comes to these combustible images. Believe me, your adoring photographer will not keep these bragging rights to himself – they never do. Even if you decide to play it safe and hide the revealing evidence yourself, one day in the future (long after you've forgotten about your camera session), someone like your parents, your children, your husband, or your nosy housekeeper is going to discover your secret hiding place and be mortified when they see a layout of you in the kind of spread they never could have imagined. They will never look at you quite the same again.

> **"Just remember a beautiful picture is one thing, but a picture showing your "neenie" and your perky "chi-chi's" is quite another."**

If you ever find yourself with even one degree of fame or fortune, these immortalizing images will somehow be stolen and find their way to the Internet for the world to see. So keep your panties on and the camera off!

By the way, this lesson goes for sexting too. It is amazing how often those seemingly fun and flirty "You show me yours, and I will show you mine" x-rated images find their way to a cyberspace audience when the recipient "accidently" hits the forward button. **Save yourself the potential humiliation. Don't do it.**

Internet Dating

Yes, there was a time when the only people to be found on Internet dating sites were those who couldn't get dates in real life. But that was then, and this is now. Times have changed, and dot.com marriages are becoming increasingly common - and socially acceptable. **You can now put on your favorite pajamas and snuggle in bed with your buddies Ben & Jerry while you let your fingers do the walking in search of the perfect mate.** Surely you can cast your net in that vast Internet ocean filled with twenty million lonely souls and find one that is right for you. Heck, there may be plenty who are right for you.

Before you decide to start the auditions, you should know that men often lie about their age, weight or height in their personal profiles. Unfortunately, they may do worse than Photoshop their love handles to deceive you. Men may also lie about their marital status, their employment status or lack thereof, and perhaps even their staggering criminal rap sheets or even their names.

In the words of your mama, "Beware of strangers!" Do your due diligence. Facebook and Google are phenomenal detective tools. Use them. If a prospective date has a Facebook page and you don't see any family members, beware. Think about it. Nobody can escape their relatives on Facebook!

Protect yourself from being stalked. Create a username that is nothing like your real name. Always meet in a public place and make sure someone knows where you are going and whom you are going to meet. And never give a stranger your address or have him drive you anywhere. Don't take him back to your home or go to his. Most importantly, don't jump in until he checks out.

That said, start the casting call. You deserve a leading man.

WARNING! WARNING! WARNING!

GETTING TO THE ALTAR

The Perfect 10

If your guy notices every ounce you gain, every wrinkle you get, and makes you feel less-than-human for being all-too-human, then the natural aging process is likely going to be hell for both of you. You must be careful about falling in love with highly critical men who openly compare you to the Perfect 10's of the world.

"You don't want your guy's obsession with perfection to drive you into becoming a neurotic, Botox-chasing, tummy-tucking, pole-dancing, middle-aged woman desperately trying to keep the attention of a Peter Pan husband. It's a recipe for disaster."

It's difficult enough to maintain your self-esteem surrounded by magazine covers of airbrushed models who wear size zero. Constant criticism (especially by someone who is supposed to love you unconditionally) can make you feel so insecure that you feel forced to enter a competitive race against women half your age. You don't want your guy's obsession with perfection to drive you into becoming a neurotic, Botox-chasing, tummy-tucking, pole-dancing, middle-aged woman desperately trying to keep the attention of a Peter Pan husband. It's a recipe for disaster.

No woman can be secure with a man who thinks that only a Perfect 10 is good enough for him. Even if you are Angelina Jolie, there's always a younger, hotter version a little further down the catwalk. The worst marriage bets are made on beauty-obsessed men who don't read the fine print, but repeatedly fall in love with sexy covers.

The Biological Clock Illusion

One of the biggest illusions modern women face stems from the ongoing programming we hear regarding the ticking of our "biological clocks." **Women have been duped into believing that since they can physically have children well into their thirties or forties, they have until that time before they need to get serious about getting married or having children. What a mistake!**

Here is the Biological Clock Illusion: Just because a woman *can* wait until her mid-thirties or forties to have her first child, doesn't mean that men are lining up looking for a woman that old to have their first child. Men who are looking to get married and start a family are looking for women who are young, not women who are trying to *look* young!

> **Men who are looking to get married and start a family are looking for women who are young, not women who are trying to *look* young!**

Women who believe they can wait until five minutes before their biological clock strikes midnight to get serious about babies are in for a rude awakening. Those who wait until their mid-thirties or early forties to get serious about starting a family will often find *they* are now the ones forced to initiate a very aggressive fishing trip into the murky waters of an online dating pond where the only fish biting are either broke, over fifty or divorcees with children and a freighter full of baggage!

If you want to be a first wife and have a "first family," you need to get serious about marriage when you're young – long before you hit the serious Botox years, and long before you find yourself reading up on the symptoms of perimenopause.

A Trophy Wife

If you're looking for a really great guy, be all that you can be—and it won't just be the army that wants you. The more exceptional, attractive and accomplished you are, the higher the caliber of men will be who will want to keep your company.

Be knowledgeable of the world around you. Travel, read, and learn to converse on subjects like business, art, wine, sports, literature, economics and politics – and cooking can't hurt either! Be charming, kind, intelligent, enchanting and interested in what he has to say.

This is sound advice if you want to be a trophy wife for a man worthy of a trophy – but that's only part of the story. **Unfortunately, no matter how interesting, successful or well-read you are, a man's interest in considering a relationship with you is still largely determined by the physical attraction that registers on his primal radar, which is triggered by the way you look. Yes, it's shallow, but it's true nevertheless.**

No matter how smart or fabulous you are, you can still gain advantage by enhancing your beauty and playing up your feminine assets. Keep in mind there is a fine line in how far you go with playing up your sex appeal. Sexy is good for a wife; trashy is good for a night.

I know many of you are thinking that you're highly educated and that it's not necessary to use something as shallow as looks to attract the man of your dreams. But, do it anyway. It helps. **The competition for the best of men is tough and you must be smart enough to compete with more than just your brain.** As I've said before, you can't fight Mother Nature. The good news is that smart men like to marry smart women, especially if they're sexy, smart women.

Cavemen

Most married women I know married the cavemen who took them by the hair of the head and wouldn't let them go. The testosterone-fueled caveman is strong, confident, bold and assertive. He goes after what he wants and rids the land of rivals in order to keep the finest woman in the land for himself.

"Just a little reminder: When it comes to cavemen, no matter how strong he comes on to you, you should do your homework and make sure he is the real deal and not just some guy who has success with women who fall for that rugged caveman approach. Let the final decision be yours, and base it on the quality of his character, not the power of his approach."

Just a little reminder: When it comes to cavemen, no matter how strong he comes on to you, you should do your homework and make sure he is the real deal and not just some guy who has success with women who fall for that rugged caveman approach. Let the final decision be yours, and base it on the quality of his character, not the power of his approach.

Mr. Right Now

Many women have the unfortunate habit of staying too long in relationships with "Mr. Right Now," instead of "Mr. Right." Don't make this mistake. If he's not right enough to consider for the long haul, take a deep breath and move on. Otherwise, the years will pass, and you'll have nothing to show for it except a few more wrinkles and a lot less men in the talent pool.

The Convertible and the Sedan Theory

A red convertible may catch the eye of a man, but it's actually the luxury sedan they choose to buy and drive every day. And while it seems belittling to compare us to automobiles, the fact is that men look at women the same way. **A man of substance usually prefers class to flash when it comes to choosing a wife.**

When Men Want to Get Married

Never underestimate the importance of timing when it comes to men wanting to get married. We like to think it has everything to do with meeting the right woman, but the truth is it's actually more about meeting the right woman *at the right time.*

Men are usually not ready to be married until they're solidly on the right track with their business or career (the timing of this varies from man to man). After that, when a man feels he's ready to be married, it's often to the next "right woman" who makes him feel like a king and gives him frequent panty access.

Oh, men do like the hunt, the chase, and winning the prize, but they're basically lazy creatures and eventually become tired of the effort and expense it takes to wine, dine and chase panties every night. The appeal of marriage is that it offers a more efficient and productive way of life. Not chasing women every night frees up more time for him to focus on his career, with the added bonus of spending quiet nights at home having sex with his wife and wrestling for the remote control.

What Men Look for in a Wife

What do men look for in a wife? When men are in their twenties, what they look for is simple: hot sex in a pretty package within four years of their age. When men are in their thirties, they look for hot sex in a pretty package in her mid-twenties to early thirties. Men in their forties? They're looking for hot sex in a pretty package in her mid-twenties to early thirties. Men who are in their fifties? Hot sex, pretty package, still in her thirties. Men in their sixties? You guessed it! Hot sex, pretty package, still in her thirties! Seems so unfair – but it's true!

Most men think the perfect woman is half their age plus seven years. The saving grace is that what men *think* they're looking for in a wife often has nothing in common with the women they *actually* marry.

> **"Most men think the perfect woman is half their age plus seven years."**

Men still marry women they fall in love with, and those women are ones who have the access (or who create the access) to get close enough to register on the primal radar of those men. Ironically, the woman a man chooses to marry frequently turns out to be the exact *opposite* of the type of women he usually dates.

Men often end up marrying a woman who is not necessarily the best looking, the best in the bedroom, or the best cook, but for some mysterious reason, she's the best match for them. **Never underestimate the power of access.**

Pushing Him Off the Fence

It's not uncommon for men to sit on the fence as long as possible when it comes to proposing marriage. In fact, many women have to resort to an old-fashioned method to get their guy off the fence – they push him off on their way out the door!

One thing to know about pushing your guy off the fence is you can never be sure which side of the fence he'll land. If you want him to land on the side where the limo is waiting with "Just Married" written on the back, then leave him with the perfect Exit Speech, or you may be pushing him into a limo headed to Las Vegas with a bunch of guys who will show him twenty-five silicone blonde ways to get over you!

After you leave, no matter how miserable you feel, resist the urge to communicate with him. He needs to feel the full effect of being miserable without you, and he won't be miserable enough if he's still in contact with you. Think of it this way: Every time you communicate with him (even if you're only fighting), gives him a little therapeutic dose of "you." Any contact with you will act as a Band-Aid to help him manage his pain, and you don't want to help him manage his pain! You want him to miss you so much he comes to his senses and asks you to marry him!

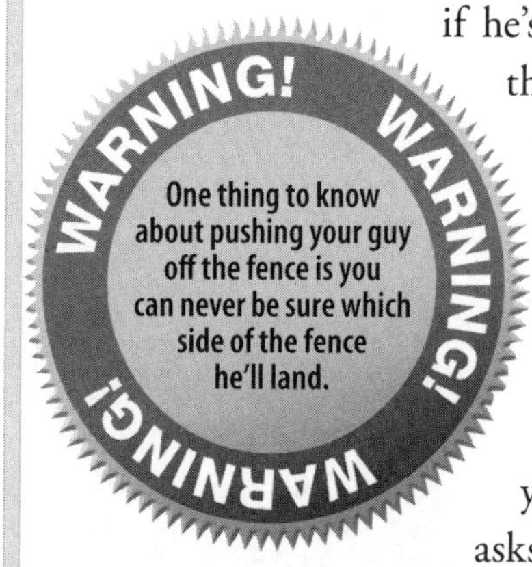

One way or another, when you push your guy off the fence, you'll be able to get on with your life. You're either going to the chapel or you're going on a date with someone else. Either decision is better than wasting time in a relationship that's going nowhere.

The Exit Speech

If you really love your guy but have decided the time has come for you to marry or move on, then don't *just* leave him – leave him with *The Exit Speech*. This speech is extremely effective as long as you stick to your guns after you use it. It goes something like this:

"I love you. I believe I'm the perfect woman for you and you're the perfect man for me. No one will ever love you more than I do. I would like to spend the rest of my life with you. But if you don't want to be with me as much as I want to be with you, in a (you can put in your own description here) fully committed, 'till-death-do-us-part' kind of way, then I have to say goodbye. I know I'm not destined to be alone. I'm going to miss you, but I'm going to go on with my life. Please don't call me again unless you want to marry me and spend your life with me. Goodbye, love of my life."

That's it. No drama. No further discussion. Walk out. Close the door. Move on with your life. Take a calendar and mark off every day you survive without contacting him and pat yourself on the back. Keep in mind that if you have ANY contact with him, the counting-the-days process starts all over again from the new contact point. **The more contact he has with you (his Band-Aid), the less likely he is to think he is going to die without you.** If the two of you are really meant for each other, then he will likely come back to you with a proposal or an invitation to step up your relationship within sixteen weeks after delivering *The Exit Speech*.

If he doesn't come to his senses, then be grateful you didn't invest any more time in a relationship that was doomed to go nowhere. The last thing you want to be doing is wasting away your days hoping to marry or be with someone who doesn't want to be with to you.

Know When to Fold 'Em

If you've been with "Mr. Right" for what seems like an eternity and he still isn't willing to commit, you may decide enough is enough and give him *The Exit Speech.* If he can't live without you, he may come back with the proposal you've been longing for. If this happens, you may feel you now have the upper hand, but don't punish him by playing hard to get. Just say "yes" and head to the altar, even if you have to go via Las Vegas in the Elvis Chapel drive-through.

If you play games, it could backfire. I have a famous friend who, after many years of living with a rock star, got tired of living out of wedlock. She finally mustered up her courage and gave *The Exit Speech,* then promptly went away for a weekend on an island with a new suitor. It didn't take long for her ex to come to his senses and decide he loved her too much to let her go.

In a gallant gesture, he hired an airplane to fly a banner around the island with her name on it and the question, "Will you marry me?" She saw it and was thrilled that finally, after all these years, they were going to get married! Feeling triumphant, she decided to show him how rejection felt by not immediately responding. It worked. He felt it all right – he married someone else three months later!

You have to know when to hold 'em and when to fold 'em, just as Kenny Rogers warned. If you haven't noticed, men don't take rejection lightly, and their coping skills are even worse when it comes to humiliation, which can be the point of no return. **Humiliation makes men do crazy things, so much so that "crimes of passion" are almost always "crimes of humiliation."** A word to the wise: When you win big, take your chips off the table and walk away. Viva Las Vegas!

Timing

Most happily married men will tell you that, when they met the woman they wanted to marry, they knew almost immediately. When a man is involved with a woman he may want to marry, his attachment is usually extremely strong about three to four months into the relationship.

> **When it comes to timing, if a man hasn't asked you to marry him by the end of your first year together, the chances of him doing so will drop dramatically.**

At this point, the sexual chemistry is at maximum intensity. This is when you have the greatest sexual power, which can work to your advantage if you want him to step up and commit.

It's a bold move for you to try to push him off the fence this early; however, if you're sure he's the one, this may actually be the best timing for you. If you're the right girl for him, he will most likely step up and commit instead of stepping out of your relationship.

When it comes to timing, if a man hasn't asked you to marry him by the end of your first year together, the chances of him doing so drop dramatically.

Give Him the Rope

If your guy is wavering or seems to be pulling away, instead of pushing yourself on him, step back and give him all the rope he needs and then some. Then get mysteriously busy. It's amazing how much less rope a man needs if you give him more than he asks for.

The Seven-Year Ditch

The average first marriage lasts seven years. This dismal situation is made even bleaker by the fact that the average second marriage (should you be so lucky or unlucky, depending on how you look at it) only lasts a few months longer. This means every dreamy-eyed bride-to-be has a fifty-fifty chance of getting The Seven Year Ditch - twice!

If you are planning to get married and don't want to find yourself on the losing end of those ill-fated statistics, then I highly suggest you both go to pre-marital counseling. **Couples who go to pre-marital counseling are thirty percent less likely to be divorced than those who don't.**

Pre-marital counseling can help you strengthen your commitment to your marriage. It will assist you in identifying and clarifying your respective marital expectations, such as: Will you keep joint accounts or separate accounts? Who pays for the groceries? Who cooks? Who cleans? How tidy do you need your surroundings? How much should you save? How often do you expect to have sex? How often do you see your in-laws? What are your short-term and long-term goals? How will you spend your weekends and holidays? How often will you go out with your friends? How many children will you have? When will you have children? And so forth.

The better you prepare for marriage, the less likely you will have to prepare for divorce.

Leaving Las Vegas

Don't roll the dice with the wrong guy. If your guy isn't absolutely certain he hit the jackpot when he found you, then cut your losses and take your action elsewhere.

A Great Ex-Husband

If you want to live the "American Dream" instead of the "American Nightmare," don't say "yes" to marriage until you are certain you are saying "yes" to a man who has strong family values and who understands the commitment behind the words "till death do us part."

If you want to find out if he is someone you should consider, ask yourself the following questions: Does he have strong family values? Does he respect women in general? Will he pride himself on being a great father? Does he have the means to support himself, you, and any children you may have? Will your children be safe with him? Can you trust him to use good judgment around your children? If you divorce him, can you trust him to choose another wife who will be a good stepmother for your children?

WARNING! WARNING! WARNING!

If you don't think he will be a great ex-husband, he probably won't turn out to be a great husband either.

Does he already have an ex-wife? Does he treat her well? Does he already have children? How does he take care of them? How does he feel about paying child support? Answer these questions honestly. If you don't think he will be a great ex-husband, he probably won't turn out to be a great husband either.

You can glimpse the character of a divorced man by what he does without a court order.

Liars and Cheats

If you marry a liar and a cheat, you will be married to a liar and a cheat. **If a person is already comfortable lying to the people he or she loves the most, then you can bet that person will have no reservations lying to employees, friends, acquaintances, or anyone else for that matter – including you.**

Rarely does a liar only lie about one thing to one person. This debate frequently comes up with politicians: Should cheating on their wives be considered when voting for or against them? Let me just say one thing regarding judging someone else's relationship: No one knows exactly what the understanding is between two people, and for all we know, they may have a don't-ask/don't-tell-the-truth relationship. If that is the case, then what they do between the sheets with someone other than their spouse is really not our business. On the other hand, those openly honest/dishonest relationships are rare in America, so you are best to err on the side of caution if the cheater has any consequence on your life.

America has seen a great lapse in morality, and this has consequently cost us all dearly in ways that will take generations to recover from (Enron, Maddoff, banks, mortgage companies, politicians, etc.) **You may not always be able to tell if someone is a liar just by looking at them, but if you know them to be a cheater, then you know them to be a liar, so pay attention and protect yourself.** Think long and hard about putting your heart, your children, your trust, your faith, your assets, your stock, your company, or your country in the hands of a cheater, because a cheater is a liar, and we all know a liar is not to be trusted.

WARNING! WARNING! WARNING!

SEX

Common Sex

My grandmother once said to me, "I don't know why people think sex is so special. Birds do it, bees do it, fat people do it, skinny people do it, pretty people do it, ugly people do it – even people dumber than rocks do it. There is no reason for people to make such a big deal about sex."

Grandma had a valid point. Sex is a baseline common denominator for all people. Everyone does it! We also eat, sleep, and go to the bathroom! You don't want to make decisions that determine your destiny based on those common elements either!

It's already a tough enough world for women. Don't make the mistake of making such a big deal about sex that you run your life around it, or ruin your life because of it!

Size Wise

When it comes to size, no matter what surprise package you find, tell him he is the perfect size for you. I'm pretty sure you won't go to hell for a little white lie like, "Oh my gosh! I wouldn't want anything bigger!" The point is, never express even an inkling of dissatisfaction for something so fundamentally unchangeable. It's a mistake that no amount of apologizing or backtracking can ever undo.

The Toothbrush Theory

Like brushing your teeth, when you're married there are certain things you have to do – even if you're tired. Yes, I'm referring to some form of sex here – whatever works, even the kind some think doesn't count as sex. It counts when you're tired and he's not. Just do it!

How long does *it* really take? We all know the answer. Not long if you stop wasting time complaining about being exhausted or feigning a headache while he tries talking you into the mood. It's a simple solution: The better "job" you do, the faster you go to sleep, or the faster he goes to sleep and you take possession of the remote control.

> **It's a simple solution: The better "job" you do, the faster you go to sleep, or the faster he goes to sleep and you take possession of the remote control.**

If you put it in perspective, it's a rather small job with a big payoff. The better you take care of business at home, the less likely he is to be looking for a temp to fill in.

> Women need a reason to have sex.
> Men just need a place.
>
> —BILLY CRYSTAL

Naughty, Naked and Nervous

Are you having first-night jitters about someone new seeing your naked body? Start with the bare essentials like a good bikini wax and a good fake tan. Waxing eliminates the risk of an unsightly razor rash, and a good tan gives the illusion of being five pounds thinner – an instant aphrodisiac for most women!

You also want to make sure you're wearing pretty panties and a matching bra. Modern men have been programmed by Victoria's Secret to expect when a woman undresses that she will be wearing sexy, matching lingerie. Seeing you in Victoria's Secret lingerie subconsciously signals a man's brain to associate you with the beautiful women in their catalog that he fantasizes about. This Pavlovian conditioning triggers an emotional response akin to hitting the jackpot, which is what you want him to feel.

Remember the power of first impressions and save your everyday bra and panties for every *day.* Even then, Victoria's Secret has you covered, so there's never an excuse for getting caught off-guard wearing mismatched undies, which may remind him of his saintly mother – or worse, his ex-wife! It's hard to feel smokin' hot when you're not looking your best, and the hotter you think you look, the more sexy and confident you'll be – and that's the *real* attraction for any man! So go find yourself the closest Victoria's Secret and let them help you build a lingerie wardrobe to enhance your glorious assets so that you look pretty all over and feel sexy all under.

Don't be nervous. Guys are mostly grateful you're going to do it in the first place! **By the time you get between the sheets, the only thing men are really thinking about is how you make them feel or if the Viagra is going to work.** So relax, enjoy, and proceed as if he is "Mr. Right"– at least for tonight.

Very Best Sex

Most married people will tell you they didn't marry the best sex they ever had. Having wild and crazy sex is great when you date someone you don't see every day, but most people don't want to have that as their everyday standard for marriage.

Couples who center their relationship around mind-blowing sex often don't know how to transition into the everyday sex that eventually comes with marriage. These couples often think that when the thrill is gone, the relationship is too, and they start thrill-seeking elsewhere.

WARNING! WARNING! WARNING!

If it's great sex you're looking for, don't assume you'll find it with the best looking guys.

If it's great sex you're looking for, don't assume you'll find it with the best looking guys. I have many friends who say the best sex they've had was with short, bald men you'd never expect to be so hot. The theory is that the prince who looks like a frog tries harder to please – Yo, Lex Luthor! Over here!

I admit it's tempting to wish for the perfect boss — the perfect parent - or the perfect outfit. But maybe the best any of us can do is not quit, play the hand we've been dealt, and accessorize what we've got.

— CARRIE, *SEX AND THE CITY*

The Joy of Sex Toys

Thank goodness women don't have to rely solely on men to take care of business between the sheets! Fortunately, these days there are tools that can help you cope with the inconsistent batting average of men: sex toys! These little mechanical wonders act like steroids for the home-run challenged.

Plenty of women find sex toys helpful when their significant other turns out to be less than significant in bed. Stashed away in the closets of many women are home-run hitters like The Magic Wand or The Rabbit. These two hall-of-famers can always be trusted to finish the game, even if you have to slip out of bed at the sound of the first snore for a little one-on-one.

> **"Plenty of women find sex toys helpful when their significant other turns out to be less than significant in bed."**

If you already have a fairly confident base-hitter, he may be able to handle some assistance from a second-string line-up that's a little less intimidating – like the *Pocket Rocket, The Trojan Vibrating Touch, Fukuoku 9000,* or the *Big O Ring.* These tiny little battery-operated wonders can help your guy easily hit a home run while still allowing him to feel like the most valuable player on the team.

> The best sex I have ever had was with my vibrator.
>
> —EVA LONGORIA

Viagra: A Blessing or a Curse

So, the mister's little blue pill is now his little blue blanket? This isn't always a bad thing, particularly if you've spent too many years with a three-minute man. However, having this new and improved power tool has inspired many men to plunge full "schwing," into a mid-life crisis clutching a bottle of Viagra in one hand and some bimbo in the other!

Sure, all men pretend they don't use Viagra. Please! As if he thinks you won't notice the difference when he suddenly wants to do it twice in a row or starts doing party tricks with his penis – of course you'll know! Just try not to laugh in his Viagra-flushed face when you pretend you don't notice his metamorphosis. Then praise him for always being such an amazing lover!

> **As if he thinks you don't notice the difference when he suddenly wants to do it twice in a row or starts doing party tricks with his penis – you'll know!**

You must remember to compliment your guy on his sexual prowess, or he might start saving his precious blue pills for someone who will. Besides, after so many years of limping along with a three-minute man, you're probably in the mood to enjoy a few party tricks yourself!

> The nice thing about Viagra is that they are proving men can go blind on it, so you can gain weight and have a great sex life.
>
> —JOAN RIVERS

Bread and Butter Sex

Food, clothing, shelter, love and sex are all fundamental needs of the human species. In a busy world where the days are long and the nights are short, Bread and Butter Sex can be the sustenance of a marriage.

"Think of Bread and Butter Sex as basic nutrition for marriage."

There are times for romance and being a sex goddess, but when you are a busy person with little time and less energy, there is something important to be said about the ability to have good, straightforward, mutually-satisfying Bread and Butter Sex to keep you connected.

Think of Bread and Butter Sex as basic nutrition for a good marriage.

The Corner Theory

Never say "no" to sex with your husband. There is always someone waiting around the corner with her panties around her ankles.

Clinton lied. A man might forget where he parks or where he lives, but he never forgets oral sex, no matter how bad it is.

—BARBARA BUSH

WARNING! WARNING! WARNING!

MARRIAGE

Wake Up Cinderella

Ladies, I hate to burst your bubble with the truth, but there is something you need to know if you haven't already figured it out: The fairy tale ending to women's liberation has ultimately turned out to be just that – a fairy tale. With all our liberation, somehow the 21st century has thrown us a curve ball and we are going to have to figure out a new plan.

Yes it is true, women in America have come a long way. We now have freedom and choices that were once only a dream. We have equal rights and opportunity in the workplace. We comprise almost 50 percent of the workforce. We have closed the education gap. We can get married or not, and stay that way or not. We can openly have sex with anyone we please. We can have children in or out of wedlock, and we can decide whether to have a career or stay at home.

Sounds fabulous. So what do we have to complain about now that we have it all? The answer is *plenty*, because something unexpected happened once American men realized that women had succeeded in their fight for equal rights: **Men conceded to women's liberation by exchanging equal opportunities for women with the historic obligations of men, and out the door they went! And half of them never came back!**

How did this happen that with all of our rights, our education and our employment ranks that women with children are by far the ones who disproportionately live in poverty? **Here's the deal. It is extremely difficult for women to compete with men in an economic race – when we have to run the race with babies strapped to our backs!** We can change the environment, and we can change the law, but we cannot change our biological make-up. No matter how liberated we legally are, there will never be an equal playing field between men and women, because women still have *all* the babies – and almost all women have babies.

And now, much to the detriment of our children, women have to raise those babies without fathers. *This* must change.

Divorce and single-motherhood have become so commonplace that men no longer feel ashamed for abandoning their children and not performing their historic duties. Half the men are gone, and there is no one in the village to help with the children because everyone in the village is working to survive.

It is said that the status of women in any civilization shows the stage of evolution at which the civilization has arrived (or to which it has disintegrated). It's pretty clear the direction in which we are headed, as there are now more single women than married women, and when college educated women can earn more money as pseudo-prostitutes or selling sex on Craigslist than in the respected professions for which they were trained. These are cultural land-mines, not just trends. The fairy tale dream of women's liberation has turned into a nightmare that features intelligent women swinging around strip poles trying to get a husband, and married women secretly trying to figure out how they can attach a Lo Jack to the husbands they have! It is time to wake-up.

It is time for women to smarten up with a collective agenda. But first, a fundamental concession is in order: We must once again show respect to men, and acknowledge the value they bring to our families. We must also stop silently tolerating the bad behavior of men, women, and the forces that undermine our families. We must press for affordable childcare and flexible work that accommodates our biology. We must either be responsibly independent, making the choice not to have children, or we must make smarter decisions with whom we marry and have children. And we must work harder to stay married. If that is *impossible*, then, at the very least, women must create a powerfully strong village of support for their children. **The free for all approach is not working! Women must unite upon a mission to preserve our rights and dignity, *while* keeping our husbands in our homes and our children on the right track. The future of our families, as well as our nation, depends on changing the collision course we are on today.**

The Secret of Marriage

No one since the beginning of time has ever said marriage is easy. No one. Marriage is like running a three-legged race; it takes teamwork, commitment and a great deal of effort to compete as a unit that sticks together every difficult step of the way. You have to be extremely mindful of keeping your own balance while staying in rhythm with another person if you want to make it to the finish line with someone you love.

A lifetime of running a three-legged race with the same person is hard work. You must have a reverence for the institution of marriage to have the stamina to stay with it. If you're not committed "till death do you part," then you probably won't make it to the finish line. If you're only committed until you're "no longer happy," then you can bet you won't make it! If you go into marriage thinking there's an exit door, you'll probably use it.

It's no mystery why people get divorced. The secret is how they stay married. It's commitment. If you expect marriage will be easy, you probably shouldn't be getting married! It's better that you both expect it to be difficult and make the commitment to stick together even through challenging times. That way it's a bonus if things turn out easier than expected. A marriage is a union between two people who make the commitment to become a family, and families are meant to be together forever.

Don't Be a Bitch!

I hear women complain all the time about their guys over the most insignificant things: he leaves his clothes on the floor, bits of food in the sink, dishes on the counter or the toilet seat up. My theory is, don't worry about the stuff he leaves laying around as long as he doesn't leave you!

Let's put it into perspective. You're married to a guy who loves you, works hard, would slog through mud, climb over rubble, or step in front of a train to save your life, and you're complaining about socks on the floor? Don't be a bitch! Just pick them up. How long does it take to pick up a sock, load the dishwasher or overlook something insignificant? Thirty seconds, that's it. Thirty seconds for someone who, in all likelihood, is the only person in the world who would risk his life to save yours.

Men are very simple. They want sex, they want food, they want to be listened to, and they don't want you to be a bitch all the time! Cut them some slack. If you don't complain so much, then he won't avoid you and start talking to someone else, which leads to dining with someone else, which leads to sex with someone else, which leads to marrying someone else.

"If you don't complain so much, then he won't avoid you and start talking to someone else, which leads to dining with someone else, which leads to sex with someone else, which leads to marrying someone else."

Unless you have George Clooney waiting in the wings, start with the fundamentals of keeping your marriage together. Feed him, $#&% him, and don't complain so much about him!

Grateful Wife Mantra

At least I have one to complain about. At least I have one to complain about. At least I have one to complain about... Frequently repeating The Grateful Wife Mantra is a good way to center yourself when your husband is driving you crazy because he doesn't help out or listen to you or understand you in the least.

Recite this effective mantra when a trip takes two hours longer because he won't admit he's lost. Recite the mantra when he insists on listening to the television so loud you think your ears will burst. Recite the mantra when he records over the Oprah special on anti-aging. *At least I have one to complain about. At least I have one to complain about...*

"Frequently repeating The Grateful Wife Mantra is a good way to center yourself when your husband is driving you crazy because he doesn't help out or listen to you or understand you in the least."

As you're chanting, remember what your single girlfriends are going through. You can also think about all those fabulous, rich, handsome, single men who are lined up around the block just waiting for you to be divorced! *At least I have one to complain about. At least I have one to complain about...*

If that doesn't jolt you into reality, think about all the single women who would be thrilled to have the husband you're complaining so much about. Now, get back to chanting. *At least I have one to complain about, At least I have one to complain about, At least I have one to complain about...*

The No-Access Equation

If you're married, you need to take this very seriously. Your future may rely on how well you understand the importance of the *No-Access Equation* in your marriage. Most men don't wake up and think they're going to cheat. It happens because of access. Here's the formula you need to memorize:

(Access + Friendship) x (Flirtation + Ego) = Cheating Dog

The Total = Heartache + Divorce

Women with too much access to your husband, adds up to no good for your marriage. I know women whose husbands left them for their secretaries, manicurists, yoga instructors, nannies, decorators and even their own best friend! The husbands are happy with their new wives and families, and the ex-wives are still not over the divorce.

Infidelity doesn't just happen. It happens because of too much access! Don't open the door for trouble when you can slam it shut. The fewer women you allow to have personal access to your husband, the better. Keep in mind the advertising campaign for speeding, "Fifty-five Saves Lives," – it saves marriages too. I have yet to see a husband leave his wife for a fifty-five-year-old nanny!

"Keep in mind the advertising campaign for speeding, "Fifty-five Saves Lives" – it saves marriages too. I have yet to see a husband leave his wife for a fifty-five-year-old nanny!"

There is a special place in hell for women who don't help other women.

—MADELEINE ALBRIGHT

Real Men

Even though we spend a lot of time complaining about men (they are such easy targets), every married man is not out chasing skirts with a bottle of Viagra hidden in his gym bag. Only half of them are! There are amazing men all across this country who work hard, support their families, help with homework and tuck their children in at night. These guys exist; they're called *real men.*

Real men put their family first. They love and appreciate their wives. They say no to cheating, hookers, strip clubs and porn. Real Men know the most honorable thing to do is to uphold their commitment to their marriage and family. They teach their children the importance of honesty, decency, morality and self-respect. They treat their wives with respect so their children learn how a man is supposed to treat a woman.

> **There are amazing men all across this country who work hard, support their families, help with homework and tuck their children in at night. These guys exist; they're called Real Men.**

If you married a real man, instead of a bad boy or Peter Pan, you are one very fortunate woman. There's nothing of any greater value to a family than partnering and sharing your life with a real man. Feel proud, and treat him right. Unless the two of you mess it up, your happy marriage will give your children the greatest possible advantage to grow up and become healthy, happy, productive members of society.

Congratulations on your smart decision in choosing a great man. Your thriving brood will be living proof (for generations to come) that all the choices and sacrifices the two of you made "in the best interest of the children" were well worth it.

No Exit

Reverend Al Sharpton presided over the wedding of two of my dearest friends. At the ceremony, he explained the reason why a marriage is symbolized by the exchange of rings. **A ring is a circle, a closed round shape with no opening for exit. Just like in a marriage where there is true commitment, there is no exit.**

Today, it seems too many people think "commitment" is like making a reservation. It suits you now, but if things change, you can always back out. Here's the secret to lasting love: it begins and ends with true commitment. When you make a commitment (as you do when you marry), it's intended to be absolute and not just until one of you changes your mind or finds something better.

Even though you may believe destiny is responsible for lasting love, it's actually choice. Not as sexy as star-crossed lovers woven from the same moonbeam, I know, but there is a reason why most poets end up broke and miserable. It's because romantic love can be fleeting. Grown-up love is rational and very conditional. Lasting love is based on respect, attraction, compromise, stability, compatible neuroses, and, most importantly, mutual commitment.

If you want love that lasts a lifetime, then choose a man who understands commitment. Pay attention to the warning signs. If your guy makes promises he doesn't keep, he may disregard his commitment to you when your marriage hits rocky ground. True love can be forever as long as your commitment is forever. Love and commitment do not necessarily go hand-in-hand. The romantic notion of eternal love not only involves the intoxication of celestial kismet, but also boring, real-life commitment, which brings meaning to the words "till death do us part."

The Starter Marriage

The first year of marriage comes as a great surprise to most couples. For some, it's an extended honeymoon, while others struggle so much they don't make it to the end of the year. I suggest all newlyweds wait at least until after their second anniversary before deciding to start a family. **A person can have a "starter marriage" and see if it works, then move on if it doesn't, but there's no such thing as a "starter child."**

> **The choice of your child's father is a fate-determining decision that should be made with the utmost caution.**

The commitment to a child is forever. You owe it to yourself and your children to make the most responsible decision possible. The choice of your child's father is a fate-determining decision that should be made with the utmost caution.

Hold off on the decision until you feel like you're making a wise and lasting choice. It's a tough world out there, and nothing gives a child a better chance for happiness and success than having two stable, married, loving parents that are devoted to each other and their children.

Equal Partners

What women bring to the partnership of marriage is not always economics, but it's of equal value nonetheless. If you don't believe this, your husband never will.

Schoolhouse Sweethearts

If you married your high school or college sweetheart, you may technically be the same age, but you're not going to age the same way – not even close. Somewhere between the ages of forty-five and fifty-five your libido will likely fizz out to a certain degree. You may not care. You may even think good riddance; you've had enough sex with your husband to last a lifetime and are quite happy to skip it altogether.

If that notion sounds a little extreme, it's not. Twenty-five percent of all married couples have sexless marriages. However, don't let the stat fool you. These are not sexless people; they're just *sexless marriages*!

> **"Sure, your husband's interest in sex with you may be declining, but his interest in sex probably isn't."**

Don't take your eye off your marriage just because *your* interest in sex is waning. You may have hit perimenopause, but that doesn't mean your husband has entered manopause. He's likely to be at least ten years behind you when it comes to a hormonal loss of sex drive. Sure, your husband's interest in sex *with you* may be declining, but his interest in sex probably isn't. You still have to take care of your husband's needs, even if he acts like he's no longer interested. It's your job to keep him interested!

Even after twenty or thirty years of being married, if you were no longer in the picture, your husband (believe it or not) could date thirty-somethings. You, on the other hand, would be fielding calls (if you even get a call) from men old enough to get into movies with a senior citizen's discount. These can be some of the most vulnerable years for your marriage. Don't blow it by assuming just because you don't feel the itch that he doesn't want a scratch.

Vasectomies

Ladies, a vasectomy is one nip-tuck you will *never* regret! If you have all the children you want, then don't spare the horses getting your husband booked for a vasectomy. Even if you think you married Dudley Do-Right, insist anyway!

Tell him you don't want to worry about getting pregnant anymore, and now it's his turn to take responsibility. Don't buy into his protests and the "castration" nonsense. It's not the painful ordeal it was years ago. It's certainly nothing close to getting a bikini wax!

The process is now practically pain-free. He can even get a no-scalpel vasectomy that doesn't need stitches. If he's a really big baby, he can also use the no-needle anesthetic technique. That should be enough to take care of all his excuses, but if not, come up with some more reasons. **Insist he get the vasectomy. You don't want to risk having your lives torn apart by some Weed showing up on your doorstep with her bowling ball belly hanging over her low-rise jeans as she gives her twelve-weeks-to-go notice.** This kind of surprise will rip the guts out of even the strongest of Warrior Wives.

Consider this: You already know the odds are fifty-fifty on any marriage lasting. Your future and your children's future will be much easier if you don't have to compete with daddy's new baby and his sporty new wife or an accidental baby with some stripper from Vegas whose name he doesn't remember.

If you're hesitating because you think some day you might want more children, then freeze some sperm and march him in! Don't wait until you hit a rocky spot in your marriage. It may be too late if he's already out the door. Don't take the chance. Your life will be much happier if you don't have to deal with the consequences if your Dudley Do-Right does wrong!

The Green-Eyed Monster

Jealousy is a powerful emotion. If it's your nature, try to tame the beast as best you can. If you can't, then own it proudly. It can benefit your relationship if used properly. How? A man's ego generally puts up with jealousy as long as you utilize it in a loving way, such as "I can't help it, honey. I do think every woman wants you." Half the time, you're right.

> **A man's ego generally puts up with jealousy as long as you utilize it in a loving way, such as "I can't help it, honey. I do think every woman wants you." Half the time, you're right.**

There is a perceptual difference that will determine your man's tolerance of your jealousy and your strict enforcement of *The No-Access Equation*, and that's whether he perceives you to be a threatened, insecure woman or a smart woman who is madly in love with the greatest guy in the world.

If you're going to own your jealousy, then own it with all women. You can't just single out the attractive ones, or he'll think you're weak and threatened by their beauty. Instead, show your strength and let him know you're madly in love with him and intend to protect him from all the women in the world who would rather be sleeping in your bed.

Your fierce love can make him feel like a king sharing his life with a very smart woman who recognizes just how worthy he is. This is how you guard the gates of your castle with a little help from the Green-Eyed Monster.

Loving Mr. Right

When the stars finally align and you wake up married to the love of your life, don't take it for granted, not even for a moment. Having a husband to share your life with is a great blessing and should be treated as such. It's important to cherish him, care for him, and treat him like your best friend because that's what he is.

Your happiness has a great deal to do with his happiness, and you can never go wrong by putting effort into nurturing your marriage. Be grateful for what he brings to your life. A good man is still hard to find. **Yes, I know, a hard man is also good to find, but with the advent of Viagra, there is no shortage of hard men.** Good men, on the other hand, are becoming exceedingly rare and so much more valuable.

If you're fortunate enough to have a good husband (or even a good enough husband), then it's worth doing everything in your power to keep him happy in your marriage. Keep in mind that if you think your man is good but not good enough for you, there are plenty of women out there who will think he is perfect and would be thrilled to take him off your hands.

Desperately Seeking Your Guy

Make friends with other happily-married couples. Don't vacation in places that are havens for singles or divorcees because they're filled with women who are desperately seeking a husband – and your husband will do just fine!

Treat Him Like a King Theory

Treat your husband like a king, and he will become more like one. Show him how great it feels to be part of the good guy club. Use terms of endearment frequently. Give him compliments, tons of them. You want your sincere appreciation to make him feel better about himself than anyone else possibly could.

Your praise should far outweigh your criticism. The more praise he receives, the less he will disappoint you. As overboard as you think you sound with your praise, do it anyway. Validate every single thing he does right. Try it, and watch it work wonders! "You are so handsome, so smart, so thoughtful, so gorgeous, so masculine, so sexy, such a good grocery shopper, such a good husband, such a good dad, so good at fixing things, so good with the children's homework..."

Men and marriages thrive on praise. **As hard as this is to believe, a man's ego is generally a bottomless pit, so no matter how much praise you give, there is always room for more!** If you treat him like royalty, he'll be less likely to run off with a servant.

There's No Place Like Home

You can't make a man stay faithful, or close to home. He has to *want* to be there because that's where he's the happiest. The job of a good wife is to make sure life at home is happy. **Remember, if you want a really great husband, you have to be a really great wife.**

For me, the highest level of sexual excitement is in a monogamous relationship.

—WARREN BEATTY

The Royal Camouflage Theory

When you see your guy walk out the door to run errands wearing black shorts with black socks or some other equally awful outfit, there's only one thing you should say, "Goodbye Honey. Have a nice day!"

Think of his unfashionable outfits as *The Royal Camouflage.* It's a great way to disguise a real prince in order to hide him from Weeds. Weeds typically hunt for obvious prey. **The eyes of Weeds are trained to scan the horizon for identifying marks such as Mercedes, BMW, Bentley, Armani, Zegna, Cartier, Brioni, county club logos, and Black American Express cards.**

If you let your prince go out wearing *The Royal Camouflage*, you can run your own errands without worrying that Weeds will readily spot him as a target on their afternoon hunting expedition. I know a low-key, single billionaire who intentionally drives around in a dinged-up Lexus because he doesn't want attention. And he doesn't get it tooling about in an ordinary car. Weeds usually have a clock ticking so loudly they can't waste time looking at dinged-up cars or paying attention to some average-looking Joe who isn't wearing flashy bling to attract their attention.

> **"When you see your guy walk out the door to run errands wearing black shorts with black socks or some other equally awful outfit, there's only one thing you should say, "Goodbye Honey. Have a nice day!""**

A Weed's radar won't spot a prince walking around in *The Royal Camouflage* unless he looks like Brad Pitt or they see him getting out of his new Mercedes. On second thought, maybe you should go with him to the car wash after all!

Compatible Neuroses

In a healthy marriage, partners don't have to be perfect. They just have to be perfect for each other. Marital success is often based on compatible neuroses.

Two people have compatible neuroses are when they understand each other in ways no one else can comprehend. This is the secret to how they can live happily (or at least tolerably) with the quirky little things their spouse does that would drive others around the bend.

Make a Date for Marriage

You can't have a marriage that's focused solely around the children and expect it to last. Men need more than children to stay connected to their wives. You have to make your relationship a top priority. In addition to the connections you make between the sheets, you still have to connect with your husband outside of the home.

"The goal is for your children to grow up and leave you, not for your husband to leave you!"

Men bond by doing things together, so make a plan to have a date night once a week – and keep it! Always make a point of talking about things other than your children. Travel with your husband whenever you can. **Your children can survive without you for a week every now and then much better than they will survive a divorce.**

The goal is for your children to grow up and leave you, not for your husband to leave you!

The Honeymoon Is Not Over

Long after your honeymoon is over, it will still be important for you to make time for romance with your husband. You need to schedule special time alone with him so he remembers that, although you may be the wife, the mother, and sometimes even the hausfrau, you're *still* the goddess he wanted to marry.

"It's also not a bad thing for you to remember that this great guy you've been taking for granted is still a great guy between the sheets when you give him a chance."

Some of the happiest couples I know swear by their secret, sexy rendezvous without the children. They say with a little champagne, a change of scenery and a little privacy, you can turn right back into the hot babe you were when he met you. And by the way, remembering that you're indeed a hot babe certainly puts more spring in your step as you go about your day doing the angelic duties of an earthbound woman.

It's also not a bad thing for you to remember that this great guy you've been taking for granted is still a great guy between the sheets when you give him a chance. And even if he's not that great, at least he's still *your* guy between the sheets!

The Gift of Sex

There is nothing wrong with doing something for your husband that you don't feel like doing just because it matters to him. Women do dozens of things every day we don't feel like doing just because it makes a difference in the lives of our loved ones. You don't have to be "in the mood" to show someone how much you care.

A Little White Trick

Never trick a man into doing anything. Rarely will you find happiness when trickery is involved. The late Suzanne Pleshette was the only woman I've ever known who actually fessed up to me about using a little white trick on her man.

This fabulous, fifty-something actress was a broken-hearted widow resolved to live a life without love until one day she unexpectedly got hit by Cupid's bow and fell head-over-heels for Tom Poston, her *Bob Newhart Show* co-star. Suzanne was deliriously happy with Tom and was gushing about how lucky she was to have such a good man waltz into her life when she thought she'd never find love again. As she waxed on about how happy she was with Tom, she confessed a little "white trick" she used every time they went out to dinner.

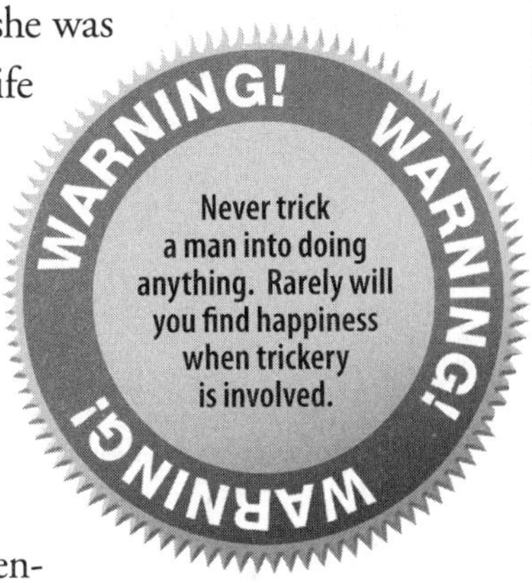

Suzanne said she always walked in front of Tom on their way to their table. The trick was that along the way, she intentionally made eye contact with every man in the room. Of course, the men would look back and stare – thinking perhaps they knew her. A few paces behind, the only thing Tom knew was that everywhere they went, men's heads would turn to watch his beautiful wife walk by, and he felt like the luckiest man in the room being married to such a desirable woman.

God bless their loving souls! If you decide to use this little "white trick" in your own life, then you really need to make sure you hide this book from your guy. There are some things men are never meant to know.

Happy Birthday, Baby

Some women have husbands who always seem to buy the perfect gift. You, on the other hand, seem to be the only one on the block with a clueless husband who sets out to buy you a fabulous birthday present and comes back with a water-proof shower radio from Bed Bath and Beyond, or ill-fitting lingerie that a truck-stop stripper wouldn't wear. What can you do?

This time, just say thank you. Next time, take a lesson from women who always get what they want for their birthdays. You don't really think their husbands are smarter than yours, do you? Don't let these women fool you because their husbands aren't smarter than yours – they're just better trained!

These women don't take chances on receiving a stupid gift. Instead, they pre-shop for the gift themselves! Just go to your favorite store and select a couple things that strike your fancy and have the salesperson put it on a wish list for you. Then send your dutiful husband to the store where your favorite salesperson will help him with a few suggestions.

"He'll come home with the "perfect gift," and you get to brag to everyone about the wonderful birthday surprise your husband gave you while praising him to the moon in front of the world."

He'll come home with the "perfect gift," and you get to brag to everyone about the wonderful birthday surprise your husband gave you while praising him to the moon in front of the world. He will feel like a king, and you'll get what you want. That's how the smart ladies do it. **Sometimes, you have to make a man a hero.**

The Green Grass Theory

Women waste a lot of time thinking about the grass on the other side of the fence. They don't realize the grass only *looks* greener. No one has it all, even if it looks like they do. They may have things you don't have, but they still don't have it all, all the time. What you may not realize is that no one is on a cakewalk, but many pretend to be. The grass isn't greener on the other side of the fence; it's greener where you water it!

Russian Roulette

After a happy stint on marital cruise control, a lot of women take their marriage for granted. They let their weight go up, they lose interest in sex and they don't travel with their husbands anymore.

A wife's neglect is often the beginning of her husband's string of affairs, which is usually the beginning of the end of her marriage. Don't assume your life will always be the same even if you've been married for twenty or thirty years. I know men in their seventies who have walked out on their wives.

"When a husband leaves his wife, it's rare that divorce makes *her* life better."

There are no sure bets in marriage. When a husband leaves his wife, it's rare that divorce makes *her* life better. If you don't put in the effort to nurture your marriage, be forewarned that you are playing a dangerous game of Russian Roulette. Maybe you'll get lucky – or maybe you won't.

Part of the Solution

If you are not part of the problem in this world you can certainly be part of the solution. There are countless things you can do to help put America back on track.

If you're healthy, loving, stable and on solid ground financially, consider becoming a foster parent. If every qualified person would foster a child just once in their life, the lives of countless children would be changed for the better forever.

If being a foster parent is too much of a commitment at this time, then you can become part of a village that helps raise a child. Offer to help a stressed-out mother and babysit every now and then, or help her clean her house, or take her child to the park or the zoo. If you have means, pay for a tutor or music lessons for someone else's well-deserving child. If you're married and have room for one more, consider adopting.

If your friends are in a rocky patch in their marriage, don't offer to set them up on a date! Instead, strongly encourage them to work it out and stay together. Offer to watch their children for the weekend so they can get away and reconnect with each other instead of connecting with someone else.

Don't silently condone bad behavior from friends. If your friends are disrespecting their marriages or neglecting their children, call them out on it. Nudge them to go home where they belong, to properly parent their children, to pay their child support, or to stop drinking or doing drugs. Let them know you don't support what they're doing. **If you act as if bad behavior is acceptable behavior, then your friends will assume you think it's okay. It's not. Don't be silent. A broken family triggers a domino effect of destruction.**

You can be part of the solution. Remember that an angel gets its wings every time you make life better for a child.

Lost in Translation

Millions of Americans rely on high-speed gadgets to stay connected. Whether you live in New York or Des Moines, we all live in an instant-gratification universe where a few taps on a keypad count as "connecting" with a loved one.

It doesn't take long to become addicted to the convenience of using a phone, computer or PDA to Twitter one's life away. At first it seems so simple to send a message saying "I love you" or "I am running late." But for many it becomes so addicting, they choose to text every occurrence in their life, from the mundane to the serious. There is a reason why Blackberrys are called Crackberrys.

People actually use gadgets to discuss everything, from what to do about their child's drug experimentation to whether they should buy a house, have a baby or get divorced. What they don't realize is this quick way of connecting is actually disconnecting them from their loved ones.

"Trying to explain life's complexities on a little keyboard can cause your true feelings to be lost in translation and deep connections to be lost forever."

It's best to communicate deep feelings of love, gratitude, and grievances face-to-face. There is no substitute. Trying to explain life's complexities on a little keyboard can cause your true feelings to be lost in translation and deep connections to be lost forever.

The single biggest problem in communication is the illusion that it has taken place.

—GEORGE BERNARD SHAW

I Am Your Wife

A wife plays a crucial role in a successful marriage and happy family. If you're a good wife, you're within your rights to expect your husband to treat you with respect.

Allowing your husband to disrespect you is not something you should get accustomed to doing. You must be strong enough to stand your ground and demand respect if your husband gets out of line.

> **"Remember the person you're fighting with loves you, so be kind, fight fair and when the fight is over, let it stay that way. Then kiss and make up. Remember, the goal is to keep the home fires burning without burning down the house!"**

Marriage is a two-way street. It's not a bad thing for both of you to have a little fear. He shouldn't feel too comfortable taking you for granted anymore than you should feel comfortable taking him for granted. "I am your wife" is a very powerful statement and one you should use if he needs to be reminded to treat you with the respect you deserve.

"I am your wife" is the abridged translation of "I am your wife, and what you're doing is wrong. You need to shape up now and show me the respect I deserve, because if you don't, you're not going to be happy with what happens next."

"I am your wife." Four small words – one giant reality check.

> A happy home is one in which each spouse grants the possibility that the other may be right, though neither believes it.
>
> —DON FRASER

Lost in Marriage

After years of caring for the needs of your family, one day you may slow down and realize every ounce of who you used to be has gradually disappeared. You may not even have noticed the slow transition that took you from feeling like somebody special in your own right to merely being somebody special's mother or somebody special's wife.

When this loss of identity happens, some women panic, feeling trapped and suffocated. They desperately start looking for a way out, only to realize there is no escape short of abandoning their family. If this is sounding a little too familiar, you should know there are steps you can take to help find your way again.

Start by making a commitment to reclaim your identity separate from that of "mother" and "wife." Be proactive. Change your routine and enter into a weekly activity that's just for you. It can be anything that stimulates your mind, rekindles your passion or soothes your soul. Maybe it's a class, lecture, job, social club, sport or starting a hobby. Go out with a friend once a week, even if it's just for lunch or coffee. Go away with your husband overnight at least once every eight weeks.

If you can swing it, take a three-day retreat once every four months to a place you've never been. It will be difficult at first to carve out time. Your family will complain, but do it anyway; they'll survive. Don't make excuses. Find a way to make it work. Trade off child care hours or entire weekends with another mother to make it a mutually beneficial situation. Be creative.

Take time to care for yourself. Don't wait until you self-destruct and the only choice is between your marriage and your sanity. Remember, happy wife, happy life. When mama is happy, the whole family is happy!

Warrior Wives

Warrior Wives are highly intelligent, fiercely protective, courageous women whose passion, love, devotion, and loyalty to their family fuels a super-human strength to go fearlessly into battle in order to protect their marriage and keep their families intact.

Marital Combat

Sharing a home and a life with another person is never easy. Conflict is a part of nature that can't be avoided. I've found that couples who communicate with compassion tend to last while couples who lack conflict resolution skills have a hard time surviving.

Doomed couples tend to act out in destructive ways. They shut down emotionally, bully their spouse, play mind games, have affairs or simply tune in to nothing but television. Some may become passive-aggressive, openly hostile, or create an ongoing level of abuse that's ultimately intolerable. If you want to make sure your marriage doesn't turn into a marital death match, take to heart the following *Rules of Marital Combat*:

No Sandbagging – Don't choose the moment your spouse has a complaint to launch "issue missiles" you've kept in storage.

Have Compassion – Remember, if all your dreams haven't come true, his probably haven't either.

Don't Sweat the Small Stuff – Pick your battles wisely.

Happy vs. Right – Would you rather be right or be happy? For sanity's sake, sometimes proving your point just isn't worth it.

Never use the "D" word – If you start batting the "divorce" word around as an option, it may well become one.

Don't Hit Below The Belt – Only the two of you know where not to land a punch.
Dig In – Establish the fact that you're committed and not leaving.
Reinforcements – Call in a therapist or a marriage counselor if you need better tools to manage your disagreements.
Love Every Day – You'll need reserves of fondness and devotion to sustain you through the rough patches.
Make Peace – When it's over, it's over. In my marriage, arguments always end with a smile and the words, "Let's stay together." Remember the person you're fighting with loves you, so be kind, fight fair and when the fight is over, let it stay that way. Then kiss and make up. The goal is to keep the home fires burning without burning down the house!

Through humor, you can soften some of the worst blows that life delivers. And once you find laughter, no matter how painful your situation might be, you can survive it.

—BILL COSBY

At the Mercy of Men

In this country – and in every other country in the world – millions of women go through their lives at the mercy of men. They feel stuck, and much of the time that's exactly what they are – stuck, trying to survive, and making the best out of a challenging life. Feminism has brought us a long way in terms of equal rights and economic opportunity; however, the fact remains that women still don't make dollar-for-dollar in comparison to men.

Sexual harassment still abounds in the workplace, and general disrespect abounds in countless homes. Here is one secret that is no secret to any woman who finds herself being dominated, disrespected, or humiliated by her husband: Women hate being at the mercy of men—as in really hate! This world is filled with women doing what they have to do to survive and take care of themselves and their children. Women are perfectly aware of the societal double–standard. **Women know all too well about the "What happens in Vegas stays in Vegas" mantra of the men, because it happens in every other city too.**

Women all across the world feel forced to subjugate themselves in order to preserve the foundation of their families, and it's not easy! But they do it anyway, because many women don't have much of a choice this side of using food stamps or living on welfare with their children. So they begrudgingly, but willingly, pick up after men who are slobs. They make dinner for men who never say "Thank you." **They have sex with the men who cheat on them with hookers or Weeds and they shamefully seek treatment for STDs they didn't get from a toilet seat. Women hate being at the mercy of men!**

Women hate being economically at the mercy of men when they have to ask their husbands for money, just as they hated having to ask their fathers for money. They hate having to justify and account for every penny they spend. They hate being at the mercy of a husband whose attitude is that because he "makes the money" (or makes more money) that he's more important and what he says goes.

Women across the world have had to sacrifice their own dreams and desires in order to protect and properly care for their children. Is it always worth it? Is there a choice for most? Many good mothers will do just about anything in order to do what is best for their children. Unfortunately there can be a dark side to motherly sacrifice that forces women to stay at the mercy of men. No matter what the reason, women hate being at the mercy of men! The desire for independence is one of the greatest motivational factors behind many successful women.

If you are at the mercy of an abusive man, you have to get out. There will never be a good time.Call The National Domestic Violence Hotline at 1-800-799-SAFE, for guidance. Men who will beat you or your children may one day kill you or your children.

If you're young and not at the mercy of men, good! Stay that way and make smart decisions for your future. If you're going to have children, marry a worthy man – and still have a back-up plan. If you're a Cleo and have managed to bypass being at the mercy of men, then a hearty high-five to you! You are a hero and a role model to the rest of the women in the world.

If you are stuck living at the mercy of a man, remember that you sadly have plenty in common with women all over the world. Know that women who aren't in your shoes have compassion for your sacrifice and respect for your endurance. Respect yourself for being a strong, smart, capable woman who is making some tough choices for the well-being of your family. You may be at the mercy of a man (for now), but even he can't steal your soul.

God bless the woman who is at the mercy of men. And God bless the man when she isn't at his mercy anymore!

To Work or Not to Work

Most stay-at-home moms will tell you it's a luxury and a privilege to stay at home and raise their children. That's true, as long as you stay married and your husband holds up his end of the deal.

When you choose to stay home to raise children, you're taking a gamble that puts the financial future of you and your children solely in the hands of your husband. You need to gamble on the right horse because you stand a fifty-fifty chance of being divorced while your children are still young.

If you opt to be a stay-at-home mom and later find yourself a single mother, how will you support your family? You need to think about this before you decide to have children and totally give up your career.

If you take three years off from your career, it translates to a thirty-seven percent decrease in your earnings, as compared to women who choose to stay employed. Also keep in mind, single mothers only earn an average of 60 cents to a man's dollar, which is why they so often depend on welfare to be their partner in supporting their children. **Another sobering statistic is that single mothers are the number one demographic living in poverty in America – which proves a lot of women miscalculate their ability to support their children when things go wrong.**

If you get divorced, your husband will have to pay support, but child support is merely that. It's seldom enough to sustain yourself, your home and your family. Alimony may help, but in most states alimony only lasts half of the duration of your marriage. Even if you've been married for more than ten years, lifetime alimony is becoming a rarity in these challenging economic times.

So don't gamble with your future. Choose your husband well. Keep at least a toe in your career, and most importantly, if you want to enjoy the privilege of staying home to raise your children, make it your job to keep your marriage a top priority.

The Status Symbol of Marriage

Let me make a prediction for this country: A few years from now, a stable marriage will be a status symbol every bit as prestigious as having a job!

As more people realize that our economically-challenged nation is also facing a major "family" crisis, healthy marriages and strong families will become coveted symbols of stability. Staying happily married is the best insurance policy you can have for your family's future. Staying married for the sake of your kids – really is for the sake of your kids. Be proud about it. There is no better reason to stay married!

It's very easy for teachers to gauge which children will succeed in school and which children will struggle by asking, "Are there two parents in the home or not?" **When a child has the gift of two parents in the home, it gives them a lifetime advantage, and when they don't, it's a disadvantage that lasts a lifetime.**

Some people agree with Ann Coulter on her political views, and some may disagree; however, there's one thing she's absolutely right about in her book *GUILTY*: ". . . We could wipe out chronic poverty in America tomorrow if women could just manage to get married before having children and to stay married after having children . . . Single motherhood is a societal nuclear bomb."

Sure, there are millions of exceptions, and your situation may be one of them. But by and large, two committed parents living in the same house do a better job raising a child than one can do alone.

If you're married, hang in there with your husband, work it out, don't walk out, and be proud about it. Your children are worthy of every sacrifice you make, and you will be rewarded with the pride and joy they bring you as they grow up to be emotionally healthy, happy, self-sufficient members of society.

Wrestling for the Remote Control

Men are never happy unless they're the one in control of the television. To a man, the remote control is power, much like a crown to a king. Just holding it in his hand makes him feel like he's King of the Castle.

Fortunately for our sanity, women are generally more motivated by problem solving than clutching a symbolic illusion of power. This genetic difference makes this conflict so easy to solve you don't even have to get out of bed or off the couch.

Go get yourself another television and perhaps a headset. That way you can watch *Oprah*, *Ellen*, *Rachael Ray* or *Desperate Housewives* on DTV, and he can watch football or flick around his flat-screen until his fingers wear out.

Watching television together is better for your marriage than being in separate rooms or having your husband watching football somewhere else with some Weed pretending she likes football!

> **Watching television together is better for your marriage than being in separate rooms or having your husband watching football somewhere else with some Weed pretending she likes football!**

Couples that lay together, stay together. If only all aggravations with men were this easy to solve!

> Love endures only when the lovers love many things together and not merely each other.
>
> —WALTER LIPPMAN

WARNING! WARNING! WARNING!

CHILDREN

Connect the Dots

We are now three generations past the 1960's divorce revolution, and the one thing we know for sure is that this "revolution" has failed our families, leaving the children of America to pay a tragic price.

We are now living in an instant-gratification, pop culture society where rich and famous celebrities are parading around for photographers, checking in and out of rehab, treating marriage like a nuisance, men like sperm donors, and babies like accessories – and no one calls them out on it – well, until they have fourteen kids, of course. Unfortunately for our society, young adults all across America are emulating this reckless behavior by self-medicating with prescription drugs, having "body part" sex without love, and by having the latest, greatest accessory: a baby without marriage! It is no surprise that most of these young people are disproportionately children of divorce themselves and are highly unlikely to be rich or famous. Rather, they are much more likely to live in poverty.

"What can we do? The number one thing is for those of us who are married, is to simply STAY married. And contrary to popular opinion, it is okay to stay married for the sake of the children. In fact, there is no better reason!"

Bill Cosby said, "I don't know where we lost it or how we lost it, but people aren't parenting." He couldn't be more right. The fatherless crisis that has long plagued the African American community in America has now spread across the entire nation. It's time for people from every walk of life to connect the dots and realize that when children grow up with the absence of a traditional family structure, they are growing up with a lifetime of disadvantage.

To bring about this much-needed societal transformation, we must each take action in our own lives. What can we do? The number one thing for those of us who are married with children, is to make a commitment to our family to stay married. If you are not married, resist having children until you are married to a worthy mate. If you are single with children, then rise to the challenge and make raising your children your top priority.

Modern women may feel like they don't *need* men anymore, however, children still do. A fatherless foundation must be replaced with an entire village of support if children are expected to thrive. Right now, America is lined up for a perfect storm. Whether our American ship continues to sail or whether it crashes and sinks will not only be determined by our ability to turn around our economic crisis, but also by our ability to turn around the single-parent crisis that plagues American families.

> **"We are now living in an instant-gratification, pop culture society where rich and famous celebrities are parading around for photographers, checking in and out of rehab, treating their babies like accessories and their men like sperm donors – and nobody calls them out on it...well, until they have fourteen kids, of course."**

> There is no doubt that it is around the family and the home that all the greatest virtues, the most dominating virtues of human society, are created, strengthened and maintained.
>
> –WINSTON CHURCHILL

Labor of Love

People who don't want children should not have children. It's as simple as that. Children are a labor of love. Keep in mind that the word "labor" is part of this equation. Labor is not something that just happens during childbirth. The real labor is caring for children for a lifetime. It's a more difficult job than anyone can possibly describe.

If you have any doubt about making such a great sacrifice and commitment, don't do it. Never do it because other people want or expect you to have children. Children are the ultimate commitment, and the joy of having them is equal to the challenge of raising them. In fact, the job of being a good parent is actually the most demanding, selfless, and exhaustingly wonderful job ever created, which is why it takes two people to do it well. If you decide to take it on, you should be married and be prepared to give it your all.

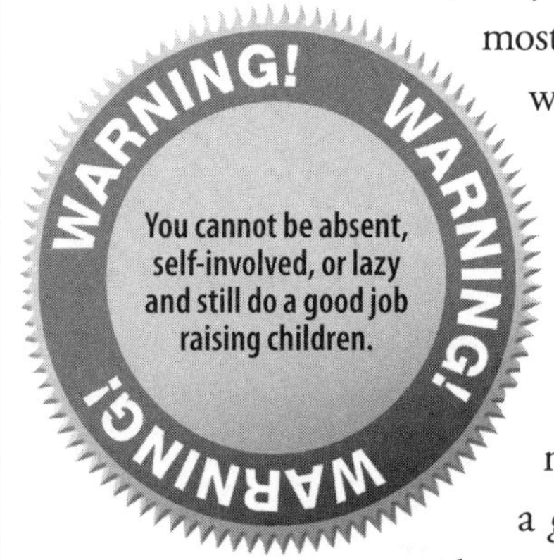

If you're going to be a mother, prepare yourself and make the commitment to not just be a mother, but to be a *great* mother. There is a vast difference between the two, and the extra effort will show in your children. Educate yourself in child development, be prepared to make their needs a priority, be consistent and learn how to discipline them without shouting or raising your hand.

You cannot be absent, self-involved, or lazy and still do a good job raising children. Be prepared to work hard, and you will be rewarded with more joy and love than you ever knew was possible. Remember the words of Jacqueline Kennedy Onassis: "If you bungle raising your children, I don't think whatever else you do matters."

Two Out of Three

Career, marriage and children. Yes, you can have it all, but you just can't have it all at once and manage to do a great job with everything. I believe a woman can do two things great at one time, and those things are being a great wife and having a big career, being a great wife and a great mother, or being a great mother and having a big career.

> **Career, marriage and children. Yes, you can have it all, but you just can't have it all at once and manage to do a great job with everything.**

It's next to impossible to be great at all three at the same time. Something will have to be sacrificed – either your husband's needs, your children's needs or your career. None of these will get your full attention if you have to do all three – and forget about *your* needs!

If you made the choice to have children, being a great mother should always be a priority. So the tough choice is between sacrificing being a great wife or having a great career. If you sacrifice your marriage, you will ultimately sacrifice your family. Although you may attempt to be Superwoman, the impossibility of the task will likely rear its head further down the line as problems develop in your marriage, your family or your career.

As a modern woman, you may not have any other choice but to try to do all three. If this is the case, you may have to concede you can't do a great job at everything – and that's okay. You can only do the best you can. Be satisfied if you are doing a great job with your children and a "good enough" job with everything else, and rotate your greatness to where it's needed the most.

Wanna Be a Baby Mama?

So you wanna be a baby mama for a man who loves you enough to sleep with you but not enough to marry you? You are kidding, right? You should think long and hard about what you're getting into. Being a baby mama is not necessarily going to make baby daddy change his mind and want to marry you.

It's an emotional hardship for children to grow up knowing their father didn't love their mother enough to marry her and didn't love them enough to want to be with them every day. Even with little ones, there are no secrets, for they always know the truth deep-down. Baby mama status is going to be an emotional roller-coaster for you and your child. Without a strong commitment to you, your baby daddy is likely to come in and out of your lives when it suits him.

Your baby daddy may totally neglect the two of you, or worse, he may petition to get joint custody. He may be thrilled to have a baby in his life, but his new wife, girlfriend or other baby mama may not feel the same way. She may be jealous and mistreat your baby, and you may never know if bruises don't show. Your baby daddy will have to pay child support, but that won't be enough to support your single-parent family.

Don't believe what you see in the media because dating when you have a little darling at home isn't easy even if you look like Heidi Klum. Even then, finding a solid family man like Seal (without a freighter full of baggage belonging to ex-wives and other children) who will cherish you and love your baby as his own is harder than you think.

The bottom line is that your baby deserves to have *two* parents, and you deserve to share your life with someone who loves you and is proud to call you his *wife* and not just his *baby mama*.

Budgeting for Baby

Having a baby is the biggest decision you will ever make. It should not be left to chance. Until you plan to have a child, you must be vigilant about birth control. Pregnancy does not "just happen" by accident; it happens because of irresponsibility, or it happens by design. You cannot leave this responsibility up to men! Having a baby (or not) is a woman's ultimate choice and ultimate responsibility.

They say parents are people who carry pictures in their wallets where their money used to be. It's funny because it's true. The cost of a baby is something you need to plan for. Do you have an extra $15,000 to $20,000 saved to put toward the baby? That's a fair estimate for the first couple of years. The average middle-class family spends over $250,000 raising a child. Surely you want your child to have the benefits of at least living a middle-class life. If you can't afford to raise your child properly, you're giving your child the worst possible gift – a life of disadvantage. It's irresponsible to think everything "will just work out." **Poverty is not something that generally works out well for children.**

Children who grow up with two loving parents have a greater advantage in every aspect of their life. Does your marriage have what it takes to last? If you're pregnant and there is no father in the picture, how do you intend to compensate for this void of support? Do you have a family to help you raise your child? Do you have the emotional maturity to be a good parent? Raising children is a moral responsibility that should not be taken lightly. Television, video games and babysitters are not substitutes for parenting.

Don't mess up the life of your child before the egg is even fertilized! When planning for a baby, be smart, be safe, be responsible and be prepared. Your child's future depends on it.

Single Mothers

Parenthood is tough. Single mothers need to do a million things right for their children to grow up and thrive. If you're one of the many single parents or you think you may become one, here are a few golden rules for single motherhood:

Rule 1: When you're not home, make sure your children are watched over by someone (preferably family) who loves them. Avoid leaving them with men other than their father. I know that sounds politically incorrect, and it may be, however it's better to be safe than sorry when it comes to your kids.

Rule 2: Stay involved in your children's lives. Know what's going on in their minds. Know their friends, their friends' parents and their teachers. Make education a priority and make their internet activities your business. Know exactly where they are at all times.

Rule 3: Don't burden them with your problems. You must be the rock in their ever-shifting lives. Your children can't solve your problems. Save your venting for a grown-up friend.

Rule 4: Keep the men you date away from your children. Make sure men aren't coming and going in your home. Children thrive when they feel secure, and that's hindered when people leave their lives and don't come back.

Rule 5: Do your job well until they're grown. Parent is a verb, not just a noun. You can't be lazy or inconsistent when raising children. Remember, there's a lot of love behind a "no." Treat your children as the precious wonders they are. Love them, listen to them, fiercely protect them and, just as importantly, have fun with them.

If being a single mother is what you're doing, rise to the challenge of bringing greatness into the world. If you do your job well, your children can grow up to be anything they want, including the President of the United States.

Mommy Dearest

You could fill several hundred libraries with all the books about raising healthy children. However, no matter how much reading you do, you can never be prepared enough for the day you find yourself tired, frustrated, screaming at your children, and crying rivers of tears. You don't need to panic, but you do need to take this moment of self-awareness seriously and commit to changing this downward spiral before you or your children do something regrettable.

What I'm going to suggest may sound like a simple solution given the seriousness of the situation, but if you follow my advice, it will change your life: Learn from Jo Frost, *Supernanny*. Episodes of her show really can show you how to regain control of your family. Jo's techniques are effective, so much so, in fact, that I believe her show should be part of a mandatory training program for every mother.

Record *Supernanny* or buy the DVDs. Watch it, study it, and make your children watch it with you. When you do, you'll all see other families in situations similar or even worse than yours. You'll learn that when effort is put in to model Jo's techniques, even situations as bad as yours can be remedied.

You can't be lazy. You have to work hard to implement her strategies and be consistent with your children. Consistency is the magic key for raising happy, well-behaved children. You will be amazed at the immediateness of the results. Think how much happier you and your children will be when you watch yourselves transform into that healthy, loving family you've always dreamed of. So dry those tears, Mary Poppins! Mommy Dearest has left the house!

Fighting in Front of Your Kids

If you and your husband argue in front of your kids, look at it this way: At least you're *still* trying to work it out instead of walking out the door. There is valor in fighting for your marriage. But I wouldn't start patting yourself on the back for a job well done. Your fighting traumatizes your children. Bickering may be no big deal to you and your husband, but to your child it means instability and maybe even divorce. If you're going to expose your children to this toxic behavior, then you need to talk to them about your fights so their fear doesn't get the best of them.

Children worry. They already know how hard it is for their friends to shuttle between a mother and father who don't like one another. Be extremely careful about using the "D-word." Just the mention of divorce can add stress to their developing psyches.

Kids will emotionally handle your conflicts better if you explain the nature of arguing to them. Let them know you may be arguing, but that doesn't mean you don't love each other. Parents argue. Children argue. Siblings argue. Parents just argue louder. Let them know that you're not leaving. Show them, tell them and let them see that you've made up. This is how children learn the skills for being married. It's good for children to see that people can argue, even in a big way, and still work it out. Don't be ashamed to let your children hear you say "I'm sorry." Your arguing teaches them that when the going gets rough, people who love each other work it out, without walking out.

Getting along with anyone 24/7 is not easy. Arguing is a good sign, as it means you both are still fighting for your marriage and your family. If you try really hard, you and your husband may argue your way through the next sixty years.

Cry Baby

When you become a mother for the first time, you bring your baby home from the hospital and lay your bundle across your bed to stare at your little miracle. A few minutes later, you hear a cry, and your heart starts to race. Is your baby hungry, wet, or tired? Does the baby have gas or need to burp? Who knows? So you guess. You start with the diaper then the bottle then work your way down the list until the baby settles down. But sometimes the baby doesn't settle down.

Since the beginning of time, mothers have struggled to figure out what the cry of their baby means. Miraculously, someone has now cracked the code! Her name is Priscilla Dunstan, an Australian mother with a savant memory for sound. She noted after her son was born that the sound patterns of his cries corresponded with his desires. This amazing discovery inspired her to embark on a global study which confirmed the historic revelation that all babies use the same universal language to communicate during the first three to four months of life.

This language is known as the Dunstan Baby Language, and it is an absolute miracle for mothers of newborns. It's so easy to learn. Her DVD trains mothers to recognize the language which is comprised of five sounds, which are actually sound reflexes all babies share from zero to three months. No mother should leave the hospital without a DVD of the Dunstan Baby Language.

You'll be amazed how it works and how much more confident you'll feel when you know why your baby wants to cry instead of guessing. After learning the Universal Baby Language, even my daughters were able to decipher what babies are crying about in malls, airports and restaurants. Now go study so that you can get some well-deserved and much-needed rest!

Mothers to Daughters

The day will come when your daughter is transitioning into womanhood, and whether you like it or not, she is going to become a woman. It's your job as a mother to do much more than just teach her to cook, clean and organize. (By the way, you should teach your sons this also.) You should be the one to teach her about the birds and the bees. Teaching her the mysteries of how a woman's body works should not wait until she has her first period. Your period gives you a monthly opportunity to share with her how a woman's body works. The less mystery about the functions of the body, the less curiosity she will have about the unknown.

She needs to know that hormones are responsible *not* only for changing her body, they're also responsible for changing her brain, and these changes will make her *want* to be closer to boys. She needs to know that hormones are very strong, and once they're aroused, they can be very difficult to control. She should know not just to say no to sex, but also to getting into intensely arousing situations in the first place because her body is going to feel like saying "yes." That's how it "just happens," and she can't let that happen to her.

You need to protect your daughter from being bombarded with media that increasingly minimizes her value as a person and increasingly exploits her value as a sexual object. Do not kid yourself about what is happening in middle schools all over the country. Oral sex is the new French kiss in many schools. Girls as young as 11 are exchanging sexual favors for money – sometimes even in exchange for homework. You need to know that if your daughter has an older boyfriend, she will advance to his level of sexual demands. *You* have to be the one to counter the absence of morality that is fast becoming accepted as the norm in society.

Your daughter needs to know that it's of utmost importance that she protects her future by protecting her body. She can't risk paying the price of her future with an unplanned pregnancy or a lifetime STD. Drill this into her. **Every teenage girl deserves the opportunity to reach her highest potential, and every baby deserves a better life than a teenage mother can give.**

Let your daughter know that her birth control is not something she can trust a guy to handle – ever. It's her body, her life and her responsibility to make sure nothing "just happens." Your daughter needs to know a condom alone is not enough, and certainly not one from a boy who may have carried it around in his wallet since seventh grade! She, not he, needs to make double-sure an accident can't happen. Her future is at stake.

> **"Your daughter needs to know a condom alone is not enough, and certainly not one from a boy who may have carried it around in his wallet since seventh grade! She, not he, needs to make double-sure an accident can't happen. Her future is at stake."**

Your daughter also needs to know that if something does "just happen," she needs to (and can) come to you right away – not the next day, not in two days, not a week, and not two weeks later. She also needs to know that if she or one of her friends ever gets into a situation that they can't or won't talk to you about, then she must know who is a mutually designated adult she can trust to go to for help and guidance.

Most importantly, she needs to know that you love her more than anything in the world and that you will always be there for her. There is no greater love than the love a mother has for her child.

Honor Thy Mother and Father

A wise person once told me: Be nice to your parents and your children will grow up to be nice to you. Sounds simple, but it's easier said than done. I know many adults who still harbor childhood resentments against their parents as if "pain" happened last week – and these people have kids of their own! I say after 20 years, move on. Your parents did the best they could. The sooner you realize mom and dad could never be perfect, the happier and healthier you will be.

There is no such thing as a perfect parent-child relationship, no matter what you see, read, or hear about other families. Every family dynamic has its moments, good and bad. Children make mistakes because they are still developing. Parents make mistakes too. We are all human.

No matter how "in the right" you are, you can't change your past or your parents, so don't waste your future obsessing about the past. I'm not saying you have to like your parents or respect their actions, but you should respect them for bringing you into this world and *let the rest go.* If you don't come to terms with your past, you may get so tripped up blaming your parents and making excuses for your shortcomings that you never reach your full potential.

Remember, *no one is living your life but you.* You can make the choice not to be a victim, not to carry resentment, but no one else can do it for you. Once you have forgiven your parents, and cleaned your karmic slate, what you do with this new opportunity is up to you. **I know one thing is for sure – no one has ever looked back on their life and regretted all the horrible things they did *not* say to their family.**

Rich Kid Syndrome

Now more than ever, America is filled with children and adults who are suffering from Rich Kid Syndrome. This condition has very little to do with the actual wealth of parents; it has everything to do with the overindulgence of parents. People who suffer from this syndrome are accustomed to having their parents continually come to their rescue and continually indulge their every desire.

This cycle of indulgence creates a very ugly dysfunctional relationship between the child and their parents. The children learn to be manipulative and become angry every time their parents don't come to the rescue. The damage caused from Rich Kid Syndrome is often not fully realized until these kids become dysfunctional adults who require the financial support of their parents well into adulthood. These spoiled children often grow up and continue to blame their parents for everything wrong in their lives.

Children who are not spoiled rotten are less likely to blame their parents for every little thing – because it doesn't do any good. No one but themselves will come to their rescue. Children who are not spoiled work harder and are often happier with themselves because whatever they accomplish in life, they know they earned it.

If you're a spoiled rotten adult child and still blame your parents for all your problems – snap out of it! There are starving children all around the world who would travel through hell to be so lucky.

Forgive your parents for their mistakes, appreciate what they have done right, and learn to accept accountability for your own life. The time has come to grow up.

Don't Guess, Drug Test

Most drug addicts get their start by trying alcohol and marijuana when they're teenagers. Unfortunately, no one can tell which teenager will be able to hold the line at experimentation and which will become an addict.

Mothers often say, "Not my child. My child is too busy, too smart, or too into sports." This kind of denial can kill your child. When our children were babies, we didn't question whether *they* could protect themselves from danger. We childproofed the house! When they're teenagers, your job doesn't stop. *You* have to protect them.

Here is the best way to start: On or before your child's thirteenth birthday, buy a dozen home drug tests. These tests works like home pregnancy tests and can detect multiple substances including marijuana, cocaine, opiates, amphetamines, LSD and Ecstasy.

Have a sit-down with your teen. Tell them you love them and intend to protect them, and you are going to be giving them random drug tests throughout their teenage years. Assure them this is not about trust. It is about doing your job. Drug testing will allow them to have more freedom and will give you peace of mind. Give them the first test on the spot. It will shock them, of course, but this is a good thing. You want your children to know you mean business, and, as much as you love them, you're prepared to send them away to a lockdown boarding school if that's what it takes to keep them away from drugs.

Don't stop testing when the tests continually show no drug use. That's the point! Keep doing it. It's the nature of a teenager to test their limits, and it's your job to stay hot on their heels. Some teenagers may still sneak around and try alcohol and drugs, but if you do your job with consistent, periodic drug testing, they will not find themselves on the road to addiction while you're on duty.

Addiction is a lifetime commitment you don't want to make.

Mama-O-Mano

If you have a son, you must be the one who teaches him about relationships with women. He needs to know that young women are not conquests to boast to his friends about. He needs to know that his first love will not be his last. He needs to know if a school age relationship lasts more than three or four months, it is on borrowed time, and that's the way it is supposed to be. He should not create a relationship that becomes as intimate as marriage.

You must teach him that when a girl says "no," he must treat it as an absolute "no," whether he thinks she means it or not. Teach your son that he is never to hit a woman under any circumstances, even if she hits him first. In fact, he should make his exit at the first sign of the crazy gene in a girl.

Most importantly, teach your son that he cannot ever trust a woman to take care of birth control, no matter what she says! He must not risk getting an STD or being responsible for an unexpected pregnancy. **Your son must always use a condom and a spermicide, and he must flush the condom. Yes, that's right, flush the condom! Your son needs to watch "the donor sperm" go down the drain with his own two eyes.** He is never to take a chance with his promising future. Drill this in to him!

Remind him the more promising his future looks, the more he looks like a prince. Some Cinderella-Wannabe may try to get to the front of the line and sidestep having to take the *glass slipper test* by presenting him with an unexpected heir to the kingdom. This royalty trap sometimes works and sometimes doesn't, but one thing for sure is that it will always throw a Prince's royal ambition totally off track.

Most importantly, do your job well and teach him that he should not settle for anyone less fabulous than his mother!

Teach Your Children Well

Set high standards for your children, and teach them to have high standards for themselves. Make them feel that getting good grades is expected. Teach them, don't just tell them, how to perform well in school. Also, make your kids participate in team sports to give them a taste of competition. The real world is challenging, and they had better know that succeeding and winning is not easy, and it involves hard work, discipline, and teamwork. Accidental reality show fame should not be their great goal – or yours.

Don't underestimate the importance of having a family dinner every night of the week. Use these dinners to talk to your children about values and what is going on in the world. Teach them to ask questions and to question everything. Make sure your children are well informed. If you do not see to it that they are learning how to think critically, nobody will. Encourage your children to state their opinions on current events and help them sharpen their analytical ability by defending their positions. Friendly verbal sparring helps them build negotiating skills.

Foster an environment of intellectualism and competitiveness. Teach your children that if they fail, they are to immediately get back on their feet and try again. Failure is okay. Standing still is not. If you show your kids a little tough love and make them work hard and learn self-discipline from a young age, you will dramatically increase their odds of growing up to be successful and self-sufficient.

It is your job to teach your children to strive for excellence, to do their very best *all* of the time. When your children do well, praise them for their efforts; do not just give them praise for being alive and being cute. Every door in the world can be open to them someday, but they will have to be smart, hard working, tough, and principled. There is no accidental success.

The Modern Exodus

America is in dire straits. Unprecedented fraud, greed, lies, theft, and deception have brought this nation to the brink of bankruptcy and have caused us to lose faith in the institutions that we depend on. American citizens are now paying the price for decades of irresponsibility and decadence. Our nation has been corrupted. Why? Why has all of this happened? I am not an economist, but I can tell you that the corruption and deceit in America has gone hand in hand with our exodus from our houses of worship.

We are becoming a nation of liars, cheaters, schemers, and shortsighted atheists. Atheists? That's right, I said it. Over the past quarter-century, the majority of Americans have abandoned religion and have stopped attending church (or temple, or mosques). The problem with tossing out religion is that we threw out the baby with the bathwater. We not only walked out the doors of our churches, but we left our Bibles in the pews. We have disavowed religion and in doing so we stopped living by the virtues of the Ten Commandments. Now, more so than ever before in America, unprecedented decadence permeates our society.

This is a time for women to take action. I urge you to walk back through the doors of your church and take your family with you. Don't get caught up or tripped up by semantics or language of old. Progressive thought and organized religion are not an either/or equation. Simply honor the history of the traditions of your religion and obey the Ten Commandments. Teach your children to do the same. The virtues extolled in the Ten Commandments are timeless – whether you are religious or not.

There is honor in virtue and power in prayer. It's up to women to bring them both back into our lives for the sake of our families, our future, and our nation.

For The Love of Children

Making the decision to have a child—it's momentous. It is to decide forever to have your heart go walking outside your body.

—ELIZABETH STONE

There can be no keener revelation of a society's soul than the way in which it treats its children.

—NELSON MANDELA, former president of South Africa

Where did we ever get the crazy idea that in order to make children do better, first we have to make them feel worse? Think of the last time you felt humiliated or treated unfairly. Did you feel like cooperating or doing better?

—JANE NELSON

Most American children suffer too much mother and too little father.

—GLORIA STEINEM

Your children need your presence more than your presents.

—JESSE JACKSON

If you have never been hated by your child you have never been a parent.

—BETTE DAVIS

If you want children to keep their feet on the ground, put some responsibility on their shoulders.

—ABIGAIL VAN BUREN

If you want your children to improve, let them overhear the nice things you say about them to others.

—HAIM GINOTT

You have a lifetime to work, but children are only young once.

—POLISH PROVERB

WARNING! WARNING! WARNING!

CHEATING

Weeds

In marriage, just as in nature, a Weed is considered to be an unwanted, troublesome, destructive nuisance that tries to crowd out that which is cultivated. **In the world of marriage, Weeds are amoral, desperate women who knowingly sleep with married men with the goal of crowding out the wife and taking over the marriage.** A Weed is a blight to a marriage.

Weeds are maritally defective women and are rarely a legitimate single man's first choice. Weeds are incapable of getting a decent husband of their own, so they try to hijack one from someone else's marriage. Weeds have no remorse about breaking up a family – that's their goal! These deplorable women don't care about anyone except themselves, and their goal is to find a husband (or a wallet) by hook or by crook.

Weeds often find easy targets to be married men who for some reason may not be "getting enough" attention at home. Perhaps his wife has to work or is caring for a sick mother. Perhaps she's exhausted from being up all night with babies. Or perhaps she is fighting for her own life and suffering the side effects of radiation and chemotherapy. Weeds don't care. **Weeds think if they can find a marriage with a slight crack, they may be able to break it up completely.**

Stay on guard. Weeds have no shame. They have low self-esteem, tainted morals and selective intelligence. For some reason, Weeds don't understand sentences like, "Stay away from my husband, you desperate $%^&*. We have a family!" Weeds frequently slither into your life disguised as employees, business associates, real-estate agents, nannies, decorators, interns, fitness instructors, video producers or even your best friend, offering the kind of assistance no marriage needs!

Confession

Human nature is a curious thing, especially when infidelity comes into play. If you pay close attention, you will discover that everyone who attempts a "bluff" also has a "tell." When men are up to no good, they always give you a clue. The famous psychiatrist Carl Jung once said, "Man is a naturally religious being who possesses an innate need to confess his wrongs." I don't know about the religious part, but I do know about human nature and the need to confess.

His confession will not be obvious. He won't spill the whole story, but if you pay attention, the clues will be enough to alert you to impending disaster. Many times, he'll start passing on little kernels of information long before anything physical has happened.

He won't tell you directly that a woman has captured his attention, but he will casually drop information bombs connected to her, such as her name or the company she works for. He may be even less direct. He may out of nowhere buy a book on poetry or take you to a restaurant that is clearly out of his usual comfort zone. Or, he may do something totally out of character like surprise you with a tickets to see some random foreign film. That should be an easy red flag for you to spot if the only movies he has ever wanted to see before starred Sylvester Stallone or Arnold Schwarzenegger. For him, sharing little pieces of information connected to someone he fancies is like letting off steam. It eases the pressure of keeping a secret.

These quiet confessions have a curative effect. Confession is a policeman's best friend, so let his conscience work for you. Next time your husband wants to chat, stop what you're doing and listen. **If you spot these veiled confessions early on, you may be able to immediately go into Warrior Wife mode and prevent the lust in his heart from traveling down to his pants!**

Hooray for Hillary

No matter what you think of politics, all women should take a moment to thank Hillary Rodham Clinton for single-handedly standing up for every wife in America whose marriage has been challenged by the ugly face of infidelity.

Hillary stood tall under the scrutiny of the world and took the road less traveled in today's disposable marriage culture. Hillary bravely chose to face the nation and endure her public humiliation, anger, heartbreak and disappointment head-on with grace and honor. Hillary Clinton demonstrated to the world that a fierce commitment to marriage and family is a much stronger bond than infidelity could tear apart. One has to *let* infidelity tear a marriage apart, and she refused.

> **"Would Chelsea have grown up so well adjusted if she spent her childhood bouncing back and forth between two houses? Would Hillary have had peace of mind watching Chelsea be driven away in the back seat of a convertible, eating cheeseburgers with her hound-dog politician of a dad and some bimbo flavor of the week who is lobbying to shift *his* gears?"**

Think about it: Should Hillary really have tossed away her family and sought a divorce because some power-struck Weed spent ten minutes (more likely – five!) crawling around on her knees like a dog in a blue dress, trying to figure out what kind of trick she could do with a cigar! Would Hillary's life have been better if she sought a divorce instead of marriage counseling?

Would Chelsea have grown up so well adjusted if she spent her childhood bouncing back and forth between two houses? **Would Hillary have had peace of mind knowing Chelsea was being driven around in the back seat of a convertible, eating drive-thru cheeseburgers with her hound dog politician of a dad and some bimbo**

flavor of the week lobbying to shift *his* gears all the way to the Governor's mansion? You bet she wouldn't! Would Hillary have been able to pursue her own goals with such success if she had divorced Bill? Would Bill have become President without Hillary? The answer is NO!

A marriage is a commitment between two people until there is a child; at that point a marriage becomes a commitment to a family. A lot of women would do well to take a page from Hillary's book. If she can survive the most public infidelity in our nation's history with her dignity intact, you can too.

If you find your marriage challenged, remember, there is always dignity in fighting for your family. There is also dignity in not giving over your entire life because of a Weed. A Weed gets nothing but a little $%#& and a few stolen moments, and that's already more than she deserves. Hooray for Hillary!

If you find your marriage challenged, remember, there is always dignity in fighting for your family. There is also dignity in not giving over your entire life because of a Weed. A Weed gets nothing but a little $%#& and a few stolen moments, and that's already more than she deserves. Hooray for Hillary!

As the family goes, so goes the nation and so goes the whole world in which we live.

—POPE JOHN PAUL II

The Seventh Commandment

Everyone makes mistakes, but how are you supposed to know the difference between a little white lie and a great big sin? **Well let's just say that when it comes to the Seventh Commandment, Thou Shall Not Commit Adultery, I think it is pretty clear that what Jesus would do is a far cry from what Ashley Madison would do!**

For thousands of years the Ten Commandments have been held in great reverence in societies around the world as a divinely inspired code of conduct to live by. How did it happened that the Ten Commandments now have become something worth fighting for in order to have them displayed in our nations' public buildings but are no longer revered as a moral a code we strive to live by? Have the Ten Commandments just become art?

How did it happen that the word *sin* has lost its meaning? It must have been when the word "mistake" took its place. Even a public confession of doing something awful to other people carries very little personal remorse and gets met with a public response that is nothing more than a chuckle, a wink, a roll of the eyes or a flick of the channel.

People now act as if the Seventh Commandment (The Sixth if you are Catholic or Lutheran) is so "old-fashioned" that it should be tossed out completely. But should it really? The Ten Commandments considered the sin of adultery so egregious that it actually is covered under the umbrella of other commandments as well: including "Thou shall not covet thy neighbor's wife" (I assume that includes husbands, too) "Thou shall not covet anything that belongs to your neighbor" (I would hope that includes the spouse), "Thou shall not steal" (I think that also would include a spouse of someone else), and "Thou shall not bear false witness," which translates to "Thou shall not lie" – and there is never such thing as a cheater who is not also a liar. It seems to me that if adultery is considered so bad that it is covered by five of the Ten Commandments, then the Seventh Commandment ought to be a keeper!

You don't have to be religious to agree that a personal code of conduct based on honesty and decency is necessary for the foundation of a civilized society. If you are an adulterer, you should not pretend to be righteous or even an honest citizen if you think five of the Ten Commandments don't apply to you. **The Ten Commandments are not unreasonable. The Ten Commandments don't say no sex, they say no adultery. Modern day translation – If you are married, act like you are married!** That means sex with anyone other than your spouse is strictly off limits. If you are single, different deal – as long as it is not with someone who is married. (There may be rules for single people too – but those rules didn't make the top ten list!) Adultery was detrimental to society thousands of years ago, and it is detrimental to our families and our children today.

> **"How did it happen that The Ten Commandments now have become something worth fighting for in order to have them displayed in our nations' public buildings but are no longer revered as a moral a code we strive to live by? Have the Ten Commandments just become art?"**

As our country slides into moral oblivion, it seems time to do more than just hang the Ten Commandments in our public spaces and admire them as art. We should read the Ten Commandments, respect them and teach them to our children – whether we practice organized religion or not. **There is not much threat of fire and brimstone these days, but for the benefit our families it would not hurt society one bit to practice following the Ten Commandments, and once again toss in a little shame where it belongs!**

Why Men Cheat

Why is it that seemingly respectable men (like John Edwards and Tiger Woods) who appear to have it all, will risk it all by stepping out with some ordinary Weed? There is only one answer women understand – because they're idiots! Why else would men with steak at home sneak out for a cheap and easy fast-food burger! It seems incomprehensible that some of the smartest, most powerful and respected men in the world would risk everything they worked their whole lives to have – including their careers, reputations and marriages – by getting caught with their pants down with some ordinary Weed. What is *that* about?

> **Why is it that seemingly respectable men (like John Edwards and Tiger Woods) who appear to have it all, will risk it all by stepping out with some ordinary Weed? There is only one answer women understand – because they're idiots!**

Newsflash! There is a stupid gene attached to the Y chromosome. Robin Williams said it best: "God gave man a penis and a brain, but only enough blood to run one at a time." I think he got it right. There's a definite evolutionary glitch between the connection of a man's brain to the sound of his zipper.

Why do men cheat? There are lots of reasons, starting with just the thrill of conquest or having a new experience. Cheating offers a distraction from the realities of their world. For a few moments, cheating allows a man to get a quick rush of adrenaline with someone other than you – a person who, in all likelihood, treats him like a king, is dazzled by his greatness (or pretends to be), and doesn't remind him of his weakness or his failures.

There's a saying between men that goes, "No matter how hot the wife is, she's still not someone else." Don't you hate that? No matter what you do, no matter how great you are, you still can't be someone new!

There's another answer to why men cheat, and that is simply because they can! When men cheat, they're usually not looking to trade in their wife for a Weed. In fact, the women they cheat with often don't come close in comparison. The Weed just happens to be someone else who provides a different experience. And *different* does not necessarily mean *better*.

A man's self-image is attached to his virility and his wallet. This is why men go on cheating binges when they become more successful in their careers. Men also cheat when they experience failure or emotional stress, and there's plenty of that going around right now. When the economy goes down, the use of psychics and prostitutes goes up. Maybe the psychics should warn the men about how miserable they're going to be when their wife finds out about their cheating!

WARNING! WARNING! WARNING!

Newsflash! There is a stupid gene attached to the Y chromosome.

Sex is hardly ever just about sex.

—SHIRLEY MACLAINE

Cleos Rule

Cleos are those smart and fabulous women who dominate in a relationship through their power, accomplishment, beauty, money or age. Just like the magnificent Egyptian Queen Cleopatra, these women rule. Modern-day Cleos include women like Oprah Winfrey, Gayle King, Barbara Walters, Kelly Ripa, Paula Deen, Demi Moore, Christine Peters, Ellen DeGeneres, Arianna Huffington, Whoopi Goldberg, Rachael Ray, Tyra Banks, Cheryl Tiegs, Joan Rivers, Halle Berry, Vanna White and Joy Behar. Cleos don't need a powerful man to boost their self-esteem. Cleos have their own power. From bartenders to billionaires, a Cleo can bring home the bacon and share it with anyone she pleases!

Cleos are not "cougars" on the prowl, looking for sex with younger men. Cleos don't have to prowl! Cleos are highly desired. Cleos seldom share their goddess selves with men old enough to be their fathers!

There are plenty of Cleos living all over the country who are bringing home the bacon, while their significant others are pouring them a glass of wine after a long day or packing the school lunches in the morning. Balance works in life, and balance works in love. But nobody, not even a Cleo, gets a free pass with men.

> **"Cleos are not "cougars" on the prowl looking for sex with younger men. Cleos don't have to prowl! Cleos are highly desired. Cleos seldom share their goddess selves with men old enough to be their fathers!"**

A Cleo must not make the assumption that because her loved one is so fortunate to be with her fabulous self that she can just relax and enjoy a relationship on cruise control. Oh no, just like the rest of the mere mortals, a Cleo still has to stay on guard.

A Cleo still has to see to it that her less-than-rich, less-than-famous significant other doesn't feel "less than" wonderful and seek adoration from some Weed who will spend the afternoon giving the royal treatment – just so that during the middle of a siesta, she can slip out of bed and sneak into Cleo's closet to try on her clothes and count her shoes. (Trust me. She will.) Cleos, you must always remember to mind the homefront – and keep a lock on your closet!

If you're a Weed, you don't want to tangle with a Cleo. So you better get off you knees, grab your thong and your flip-flops and run! If you stay around and get caught, Ms. Cleo will destroy you. She will drop your name to her allies and mark you with a Scarlet Letter A. And without Ms. Cleo ever having to say another word, the world will show their respect to her by blocking your advancement. You will wake up one day and wonder why nothing is working in your life – why jobs disappear, why clients disappear and why men disappear. And as your years waste by, you will eventually figure it out. A Cleo rules – and she *never* forgets.

WARNING! WARNING! WARNING!

If you're a Weed, you don't want to tangle with a Cleo. So you better get off you knees, grab your thong and your flip-flops and run! If you stay around and get caught, Ms. Cleo will destroy you.

> Some of us are becoming the men we wanted to marry.
>
> —GLORIA STEINEM

Marriage Is Like Pizza

Think of the circle of life as one big pie. Maybe like one big, delicious California Pizza Kitchen pie. In the beginning, it's all yours to enjoy. Then you get married, and you and your husband agree to toss in your favorite ingredients so you can share an even better pie. As time goes by, the two of you pool your money, buy a home, have children, and your family becomes his family, and his family becomes yours. Soon, that huge circle of pie that was once shared by just the two of you is now being divided up and shared with an expanded network of friends, family and associates.

> **"The actual intimate between-the-sheets time with your husband is only the tiniest sliver of that one little piece, which is an even tinier fraction of that big pie that was once belonged only to the two of you."**

Over time, the slice of pizza that you and your husband get to enjoy alone turns out to be only a very small slice of what started out as a great big pie. The actual intimate between-the-sheets time with your husband is only the tiniest sliver of that one little piece, which is an even tinier fraction of that big pie that was once belonged only to the two of you.

A big pizza as tempting as yours is almost certain to attract the attention of a Weed who likes the looks of your pie so much that she decides she wants to steal it. However, as much as she wants it, she can still only steal your pie by taking it one sliver at a time. If you stay on guard and catch the thieving Weed early enough, all she gets to steal is a mere morsel – the tiniest sliver of a very small and relatively insignificant little piece of pie. You still have the rest (and the best part) of the pie, which everyone at the party still gets to share and enjoy.

However, if you don't stop the thieving Weed, she may eventually steal your husband – and your pie. Poaching your husband is bad enough, but stealing your whole pie is far worse! Your pie has been mixed with his for so long that it can't simply be divided without having the whole pie ripped apart and ruined for everybody. What's left is nothing short of one big mess.

WARNING! WARNING! WARNING!

A big pizza as tempting as yours is almost certain to attract the attention of a weed who likes the looks of your pie so much that she decides she wants to steal it.

The point is, if some low-life rat of a Weed tries stealing a piece of your pie – exterminate the Weed! That way, all the Weed gets to steal is a little taste – not much more than mouthful – which you won't ultimately miss. You and the rest of your gang will still enjoy the pie. No one else at the party will even notice (or care) that your husband is sitting in the corner eating humble pie, as long as he's still at the party!

The Status Of A Weed

A Weed will always be a Weed to an ex-wife. A Weed ceases to be a Weed to the rest of the world when she turns into a wife.

> Being a woman is a terribly difficult task, since it consists principally in dealing with men.
>
> —JOSEPH CONRAD

Tumble Weeds

Sometimes women who find out about a Weed encounter ask the question, "What does she have that I don't? What does she have that makes her so special?" Sometimes men also mistakenly assume that because of the company she keeps (between the sheets) that she must have something special going on. So what does she really have that is so special? Nothing. That is unless you think readily saying "yes" to sex with a bunch of guys makes you special. If she were really so special, one of those guys would be married to *her*!

If you easily say "yes" to sex with no strings attached, you could tumble in and out of bed with plenty of married men, or any men, for that matter. That doesn't make you more of a woman: it makes you a Tumble Weed! A Tumble Weed understands exactly what she's doing. (See *Home-Wreckers 101.*) She uses the very effective, "everyone wants me" ploy to manipulate a slew of men into competing for her attention, hoping that one will fall for her tricks, turn into a caveman and muscle her away from her other suitors.

Men are slow to understand that a Weed uses the "everyone wants me" ploy as a setup to give the illusion that she's a prize. She knows the hunter's rule: "If there isn't a prize, it isn't worth winning." So she creates competition by saying "yes" to many men, which leads every man to think he might get lucky, and he just might. Men revel in being in a &#$% contest with other men. Men delight in behaving like dogs and marking their territory to show where they've been. Talk about male bonding! What does she have that you don't? A reputation you wouldn't want.

In the end, men rarely marry Weeds who have been marked so many times, except for the really stupid men who find out soon enough that the habit of saying "yes" is a hard one to break!

Cyber Temptation

Modern technology makes it simple for someone you thought was in your past to reconnect with you at the push of a button. Too much time being intimate with a keyboard and connecting with "long-lost friends" can be a disastrous for a marriage.

Before the proliferation of social networking sites like MySpace and Facebook, it took a little effort to find a cheating partner, but not anymore. Cyber-theft of relationships is becoming increasingly common. Long-forgotten lovers can be tracked down with a few clicks, while people you've never met before can become instant new "friends."

"Every husband in the country is now no more than one click and five miles away from some Weed pretending she is looking for hot sex in the afternoon – when she's actually hoping to hook up a wedding ring or drum up some extra cash by digging her hooker heels into the back of someone else's husband."

To make things even worse, cheat-on-your-spouse-with-me websites are now proliferating on the Internet. Every husband in the country is now no more than one click and five miles away from some Weed pretending she is looking for hot sex in the afternoon – when she's actually hoping to hook up a wedding ring or drum up some extra cash by digging her hooker heels into the back of someone else's husband.

The cyber temptation that goes hand in hand with social networking can blur the lines of fidelity for both of you. **Social connections that are made on a keyboard are increasingly being solidified between the sheets.** So stay on guard. Monitor your husband's "social networking," skip the "old friend" reunions, and focus your attention on the relationships within the walls of your own home.

Weed Whacking

If you happen to discover a Weed trying to take hold in your garden, you need to get prepared to do some serious *Weed Whacking*! I suggest you get out your "ho" hoe, turn the dirt up and rip the Weed out by the roots!

Weeds follow the rules from Home Wreckers 101. Their entire mission is a patiently planned setup to incite you to kick your husband out of the house. Don't do it! It's a wife trap! Never impulsively kick your cheating husband out of the house if you have a marriage worth saving, and if you have a family, you absolutely have a marriage worth saving.

> **"Never impulsively kick your cheating husband out of the house if you have a marriage worth saving, and if you have a family, you absolutely have a marriage worth saving."**

You can divorce him later if necessary, but do it on your own terms *after* you have a better life in store or a fabulous new husband waiting in the wings.

As hurtful as infidelity is, if you have a family, you are almost always better off if you swallow your pride and turn into a Warrior Wife. You're going to have to go into battle. The solution is not to leave your husband; it's for him to get rid of the Weed!

People scorn home-wrecking Weeds. So, instead of keeping his affair a secret, you must expose it! That's right, just hold your head high and play hardball. Ask for help from the most important people in your lives: his parents, your parents, his best friends, his business partners, as well as your pastor, preacher, minister, or rabbi. Ask them to talk some sense into him. Let them convince him to be a man of honor, to get rid of the Weed, and to keep his family together. They can help shine a light on the down side of divorce and remind him that a real man does not allow his family to be destroyed because of sex with a Weed.

The condemnation from the people he respects will shame him and give him the strength to do the right thing, which is to permanently exterminate the desperate Weed and stay accountable to his marriage. Don't worry about what others think. This is your life, and if anyone is embarrassed, it should be your husband and the Weed – not you! You can be proud to be a Warrior Wife who is strong enough and smart enough to fight for what is best for your family. Remember, there is always dignity in family. There is never dignity in cheating.

Just Friends

Whenever your man starts defending himself with the words "We're just friends," then "Just get rid of her" should be your response. "Just friends" is how it always happens; rarely is it ever "just strangers."

Go watch the movie *When Harry Met Sally* and listen to the conversation about men and women being friends. Harry says men can't be "just friends" with women unless they've already slept with them. I agree. You'll gain nothing by allowing your husband's new "friendship" to continue. You have too much to lose. Don't take the chance.

If you decide to ignore my advice on this topic, then go pick up a book called *Not Just Friends* by Shirley Glass. It will guide you in the process of confronting him when you wake up one morning and realize they were "just friends" before a late night in the office and a few too many martinis!

Warrior Wife Versus Weed

You aren't finished Weed whacking until you confront the Weed. Your mission to destroy their relationship completely will be more effective if the Weed understands clearly and openly that she is dealing with a Warrior Wife. You don't need to boil her family pet or anything that insane, but establish your strength by initiating contact with her through a third party like her boss, parent, associate or colleague. Don't start with her friends, as they may be as worthless as she is.

Ask them for the Weed's number (even if you already have it), and when they don't give it to you, ask them to give her the message to call you regarding your husband. They will speed dial your message to her. The reason you contact people around her first is so the Weed knows you are strong, bold, fearless and mean exactly what you say when you speak to her. Continue working your way through your list to get your message passed on. Then call her and get her on the phone.

When you confront her, don't hold back on what you think of her. Inform her that if she has any further contact with your husband, you will make it your mission in life to tell every person within six degrees of separation who she is and what you think of her. She should know you mean business.

I know of more than a few Weeds who have high tailed it for the hills once the "crazy wife" stepped up for her marriage and put in a few calls to the rolodex around the Weed. **Even Weeds don't like to face the ugly truth when a mirror is held to their face or when their scandalous image is reflected to the people around them.**

If she's married, don't call her husband yet. It's better that her husband is stuck with the Weed he picked instead of tossing her out and having her trying to take root elsewhere. Make it perfectly clear to the Weed that her husband will be your next call if you discover contact of any kind is made with your husband, and do it if you have to.

If she really got your message loud and clear, this call probably won't be necessary. However, if it is necessary to make that call, it will trigger another ugly drama that will bring a whole other element of unsexy to their afternoon delight. Her package becomes much less attractive once it includes the possibility of a crazy husband, attorney bills and someone else's heartbroken children.

Very few women want the entire world to know they are Weeds. Weeds like to do their business underground. Look at the length Angelina Jolie went to in order *not* to look like she had anything to do with the break-up between Brad Pitt and Jennifer Aniston. Still, it took six children later before the tabloids would finally let the rumor go away. (If Jennifer knew then what she knows now, she and Brad might still be married and have two little towhead children of their own by now.)

"**Being faced with public scorn and contempt from the people whose opinions they respect the most is the surest way to cool off hot sex in the afternoon between a cheater and a Weed.**"

Being faced with public scorn and contempt from the people whose opinions they respect the most is the surest way to cool off hot sex in the afternoon between a cheater and a Weed.

A 'Bunny Boiler' doesn't stand a chance against a Warrior Wife!

> Marriage is an adventure, like going to war.
>
> —GILBERT K. CHESTERTON

After the Weed

Getting rid of a Weed is one thing, but keeping one from returning is another. It's not enough to pull a Weed out and think that's that. When you pull out a Weed, it creates a void that must be filled. Stay on alert! Weeds that have been whacked often lie dormant for long periods of time just waiting to see if a crack in the marriage opens again.

To keep them away forever, you need to seal the crack in your marriage with something strong. But first you have to understand why the crack opened in the first place. You and your husband should go to marriage counseling. Talk about why it happened and how you can go forward. Then work on your marriage. Participate in activities that bring you closer. Spend more time together. Have more sex and do things that reinforce your commitment to each other.

> **"Stay on alert! Weeds that have been whacked often lie dormant for long periods of time just waiting to see if a crack in the marriage opens again."**

It takes a lot of effort to maintain a beautiful garden. If you want to have one free of Weeds, you have to give it constant attention. If you have even one season of neglect, you will likely find the same Weed or another trying to take hold once again. Surviving a Weed infestation is not easy, but you can do it. Once the two of you rebuild the trust that was broken you may even end up with a marriage that is better and stronger than before.

Your husband will certainly respect you for being a Warrior Wife and going to battle to save your marriage and your family.

A Message to Weeds

You may think sneaking around with someone else's cheating husband is no big deal and that it's "just sex," but you are quite wrong. It is a big deal. Distracting a man from his wife and family is a big, ugly deal that is reprehensibly damaging to a family – and inevitably, to society in general. You may think it doesn't matter to you because you don't know his wife or family, but I assure you, it's going to matter to you soon.

You deserve all the scorn that's getting ready to come your way. **If Weeds like you weren't a dime a dozen, then more of the fathers in America would be spending their nights at home where they belong, teaching their children values and tucking them in at night.**

Change has come to America, and with change has come the courage for women to unite and fight for the respect of families. Warrior Wives are no longer going to keep your name or your home-wrecking attempts a secret. Warrior Wives are going to call you out for your bad behavior, and they are going to block your every move.

Weeds, it's time for you to retreat. Walk away from married men. Don't take their calls, don't receive their advances, don't flirt with them or give them the time of day. Should you choose to ignore this warning, do not underestimate the strength of a nation of united Warrior Wives prepared to battle you and undermine your advancement on all fronts – personally, socially and professionally.

Remember the wisdom of Maya Angelou: "When you know better, you do better…" Maybe you didn't know better before, but you do now. So redeem yourself by putting this deplorable behavior behind you, and go forward to lead a decent and honorable life.

Consider this your notice from United Wives of America: Weeds, you are now enemy number one!

Boy Toys

Now to the flip side of infidelity. Some of you are playing Russian Roulette with your marriages. Fortunately, your husbands are so self-involved they don't notice the obvious signs that you're cheating. This is lucky for you because one thing's for sure: If he finds out, he's not going to handle it well, to say the least!

Some of you are trying to play it safe by cheating exclusively with married men. Some of you, though, are foolishly asking for real trouble by cougaring around with boy toys who have nothing to lose if your husband finds out. Boy toys have the same motivation as Weeds. They *are* Weeds! They don't care if your husband leaves you. In fact, they hope he will. Maybe then your boy toy can move into your house and drive your Mercedes all the time.

You're making a big mistake thinking your affair is a secret. Your girlfriends who know have told at least one other friend, and some of them have told their husbands just to keep them on their toes. Another thing you can be sure of is that your boy toy's buddies know the name of the uptown girl he's boffing.

You all cite the same reasons for cheating (which, by the way, are the same lousy reasons men use). I know your justification is the old "A girl has to do what a girl has to do to stay married to a jerky husband" routine. Still, you have a lot to lose if you get caught, and if you get caught, it's not going to be pretty. At the very least, you'll be giving your husband a free cheating pass forever.

Your husband may seize your indiscretion as justification to waltz out the door guilt-free and marry his cute receptionist. You may then be stuck with your afternoon delight, who may not think sex with an older woman is quite as hot when the lease on your Mercedes runs out and your ex replaces it with a nice sensible Hyundai. Think about *that* while you're waiting for your carpool!

How to Catch a Rat

If you smell a rat and decide you're going to catch it, you have to be smart. Rats are known to be sneaky creatures, but many have met their demise when they accidentally took the bait and walked into a rat-trap. If you're suspicious of your guy's whereabouts and ask him if he really was where he said he was, it will do no good. He'll just say, "Yes, of course," and then turn the tables on you by saying you're crazy for acting so jealous. If this routine sounds eerily familiar and is starting to make you wonder if you really are crazy, then it's probably is time to set a rat-trap.

The next time he comes home late with a story you don't believe, bait the trap by devising the perfect question based on the circumstance. For example, if he says he was at a meeting a hundred miles away and you think he was three blocks away having private lessons with his tennis instructor, nonchalantly pose a question like "The television said there was a bomb scare and the northbound lanes got shut down for hours. How far north did you get before taking the detour?" Then stay "calm as Sully" and wait for the answer.

If your question was spot on and he's lying, he'll realize he's caught. You can watch it register on his face as he struggles to fabricate a story. Odds are, you were smelling a rat long before you set the trap, so I hope you gave some thought as to what you're going to do with the rat now that you have him writhing in front of you. If he answers the question satisfactorily, and you really are a little crazy, then hallelujah! Shift gears! Just bail out with something like "Hmmm. Oh, well. I was only half listening. Must have been part of a storyline. I'm so glad you're home!"

Remember, intuition is rarely wrong – unless you really are a little crazy.

Spying on Your Man

If you're contemplating resorting to spyware, then beware. What you are thinking of doing is probably illegal – as in "go to jail" illegal! As tempting as it is, you don't want to go there! Spyware is cheap and easy – and it works – really well. I take great pride in helping relationships stay together, and one thing I'm sure of is that the odds of spyware bringing you closer together are slim to none. You may find the proof you need to end an affair, but it could also end your marriage in the process.

> **If you're contemplating resorting to spyware, then beware. What you are thinking of doing is probably illegal – as in "go to jail" illegal!**

If you're compelled to disregard the law and go on an undercover mission to the dark side, you better be able to handle the truth – or the jail time. You can be certain you'll discover something that, at the very least, will tick you off and, more likely, break your heart. I urge you to think twice about going down this road.

Most men get caught cheating because of their phone records or their email trails. New technology has made an electronic trail of deceit much more common to find than lipstick on a collar. There's a stealth computer-monitoring program called *eBlaster* that can be remotely installed on a computer simply by sending an email attachment they open – such as a "Remember my face, because you're going to miss it" photo.

Other spy programs like *SoftActivity* and *Spector Pro* have to be downloaded to the actual computer. All of these products record email, websites visited, as well as instant messages and chats. There are also tiny gadgets like *Stealth iBot Computer Spy* and *KeyKatcher*

Mini Device that can be installed in the back of a computer in seconds with no software. He can secretly chat the night away, and the next morning the device can be taken out, plugged into another computer and display everything he typed, including his passwords.

There is almost nothing that you say or write electronically that is safe from the spying eyes of someone who wants to know your business. A company called *Brickhouse Solutions* has come out with *Cell Phone Spy*, a little tiny device that can instantly download the information from a cellphone *SIM card* or *Smart card.* This little gadget is then inserted into a computer and with a few button clicks there is a complete record of every number ever dialed, every contact in the phone book, and every message that has been sent or received – including those that were deleted. So far, that technology doesn't work on *Smartphones.* (Must be why they call them *Smartphones*!) Interestingly, one of the most common tricks of spying spouses is to simply seize the opportunity to check out the spouse's lowly laptop with e-mail accidently left open. They then just go to "settings" and have a duplicate of every e-mail going in and out forwarded to *their* e-mail account. Specific filters can even be set on Gmail accounts so only the ones from 'persons of interest' are forwarded.

Now that you know about *some* of the dirty tricks of spyware, be very careful. Big Brother is everywhere and may be watching you. I repeat my warning: Keep this book away from men! Otherwise, it may inspire them to use some spy technology on you! Don't break the law and get yourself in trouble. It's pretty hard to guard the gate if you're behind bars. Go to TheRealSecretsWow.com if you want to know the best spyware removal and detection programs to protect your own computer and cellphone. Snooping men reading this book will have to work a little harder for that secret!

Dirty Tricks of The Professional Cheater

Some men will go to great lengths to cover their naughty trails. These dodgy men often fancy themselves as Hugh Hefner wannabes, or they are the ones married to a Cleo who have been caught before and know they're on very short leash with their wives. These are the men who get an adrenaline rush from the Playboy lifestyle or those who don't want a divorce (especially a costly one) and don't want to give up their Weed(s) either. Professional cheaters make sure not to make careless mistakes by leaving trails of receipts, email evidence, phone calls, text messages, sext messages or lipstick on the collar.

How do they get away with it? The easiest and most common trick they use is simply that Jane Ho's number is entered in their address book with an alias such as John Nelson, their stockbroker. This way, when the number continually shows up on his phone log, he just says he's talking to his broker.

If Jane Ho knows he would never marry her, even if he were divorced, then she may conspire with him to hide his cheating from his wife and keep her good gig going. In this case, she usually carries a hotline cell phone just to receive his calls. If you call the number, it will play a recorded message from this "John Nelson" saying he is away from his desk and to leave a message.

Jane Ho knows when the phone rings that she should pick it up but never speak first. If you want to try to figure it out, you may be able to get Jane Ho to talk by getting a voice disguiser to make your voice sound like a man's voice, which may be enough to get her to speak and tell you to stop calling – you have a wrong number.

Hopefully, she won't turn out to be one of your friends! You may also be able to find out the identity of the mysterious blocked number that registers at all hours, by calling on a company like the National Network of Private Investigators. Generally, if they don't find the name it is registered to, you don't pay for the service.

If you don't mind being featured behind bars in an episode of *Snapped*, you could (illegally) find out how his new temp is handling her job duties by accidentally leaving *The World's Smallest Wireless Camera* or the voice-activated *Mega Mini Spy Camera Stick* in his office. If you want to know if his late night is really in his office, you could (illegally) monitor his whereabouts via telephone by installing, connecting and hiding the icon for the GPS application *Loopt* or *Google Mobile Latitude*. If you don't have access to his phone, you can toss the eighteen-day battery-operated *GPS Vehicle Tracker* or *Bolt AVL Fleet GPS Tracker* under the seat of his car. Your computer can monitor every location the car has been on a street map, noting the address where he spent his day (or night), for how long and at what time. You can even get real time message alerts for location changes.

"There's a lot to be said about enjoying life with someone you don't need to put a LoJack on!"

But remember this: If he's gone to such trouble to stay married to you, are you sure you want to know? On the other hand, if your kids are grown and you have heard enough lies to last a lifetime and there is plenty of money to spare, the truth may set you free. You could be like Mel Gibson's wife, and take your fifty percent and turn into a Cleo overnight. There's a lot to be said about enjoying life with someone you don't need to put a LoJack on!

The Copperfield

Sometimes what happens in Vegas doesn't stay in Vegas, because it's not really happening in Vegas in the first place! Enterprising husbands or boyfriends may want you to *think* they are attending the Consumer Electronics Show in Vegas, when actually, the latest state-of-the-art 150-inch Panasonic flat screen is the furthest thing from their minds. In reality, they're snuggled down at the Canyon Ranch in Arizona getting double massages and having breakfast in bed with their yoga instructor. How do they pull a Copperfield? It's very simple. Professional Cheaters always follow the fundamental rule from Cheaters 101: Never carry a camera phone. That way they can never be asked to instantly prove where they are or whom they are with. You can't even ask them to show you how crowded the convention center is. This foundation makes every other deceptive illusion easy for the Professional cheater.

> **"Professional Cheaters always follow the fundamental rule from Cheaters 101: Never carry a camera phone."**

The Professional Cheater creates his magic act by using technology like *SpoofCard* to assist him in pulling off the ultimate Copperfield. *SpoofCard* allows him to appear to be in one place when actually he is in another. He sets up his disappearing act by going to *SpoofCard.com* and purchasing phone card minutes that allow him to type in whatever false number he *wants* you to see on the caller ID – like the payphone number in the Vegas Convention Center. Can't you just hear him now? "Honey, I know. It makes no sense that cell phone coverage is bad at an electronics convention. I had to wait in line at a pay phone just to call you!" *SpoofCard* covers his tracks so well that it won't even occur to you that he is not at the number you see on your caller ID but may actually be in a different city, state, or even country for that matter.

Then, when he wants to log the late night call to you, but dreads actually speaking to you, he just calls *267-SLYDIAL* to bypasses you completely and instead go straight to your voicemail. This way, he can avoid interrogation until the morning.

"I called you last night to say good-night, and it just went to your voicemail. Where were *you*?" Bingo! 007 turns the tables on *you* and escapes once again!

> **The professional cheater creates his magic act by using technology like *Spoofcard* to assist him in pulling off the "Copperfield."**

Obviously, cheating is easier than ever. You can use these dirty tricks too, but I hope you don't. Deception can be a slippery slope. On the other hand, if you're married to a compulsive cheater and want to stay married, then perhaps you shouldn't feel too guilty if you play by your husband's "Don't ask, don't tell – the truth" rule. In the South they say, "What's good for the goose, is good for the gander." It's only fair that everyone plays by the same rules – whatever they are.

If your husband invoked a rule-change in your marriage perhaps you don't need to feel too guilty about having a *SpoofCard* of your own and checking into the Canyon Ranch with *your* yoga instructor. You won't resent the old goose flying so low over Vegas quite so much if you take a gander at spreading your own wings every now and then!

Okay, maybe not. The truth is, tit-for-tat is a dangerous, losing game to play if you want to stay married – but I sure like the zing of the way it sounds!

Physical Evidence

If you are a fan of Melina Kanakaredes and have been watching a little too much CSI, you may decide that you actually want to confirm your suspicion that your guy is cheating by proving it with physical evidence. You can easily practice being a forensic scientist by purchasing a home "semen testing kit" from www.GetCheckMate.com.

The semen testing kit can detect stains on sheets or towels or any unwashed articles of clothing. The company says that just because you can't see the evidence doesn't mean it's not there. Men continue to secrete small amounts of semen after ejaculation. Traces of dried semen will almost always be present in undergarments after sex – even if a man uses a condom, even if he *only* had oral sex, and even if he showered!

> **Even a self-absorbed, ego-maniacally cheating husband checks in his brain every now and then to register the fidelity of his wife. If your cheating gets on his radar, it may be more than your marriage at risk.**

Be prepared for the result. They claim there are no false positives with this test. If you confront him with the test results, then you are probably going to need to use a polygraph test as well, after he launches into his diatribe of semen stain excuses such as how he "relieved himself" alone in the bathroom during the middle of a stressful day or how it was left over from his early morning shower, rinse and release routine. Basically, when used on a man, the test is only as effective (or ineffective) as his ability to lie and your gullibility in believing him.

On the other hand, this test is extremely effective when used on wandering wives. Your usually lazy husband may decide to skip the sniff test and instead opt for a little midnight laundry surfing to retrieve and test those cute little ruffle panties you tossed off when you came home from your late "night out with the girls." If he gets a positive response, you better hope the guns are out of the house. I am not kidding. Midnight jealousy makes people crazy and there is no way *you* are going to be able to lie your way out of a positive result.

These tests are as readily available for him as they are for you. I suggest you take this warning very seriously. Catching a woman cheating is not difficult. Even a self-absorbed, ego-maniacally cheating husband checks in his brain every now and then, to register the fidelity of his wife. If your cheating gets on his radar, it may be more than your marriage at risk.

If this is you – you had better hide this book away before it tips him off to the fact that there is even such a thing as a semen detection kit. If you don't hide this book, then you better take precautions and tell your polo player it's time to saddle up and ride his hot body over to another stable.

Deny Till You Die

If you ever make the mistake of cheating on your husband and you want to stay married, the age-old rule holds true: "Deny till you die." Don't confess to your husband just because you feel guilty. (Find yourself a priest and ask forgiveness in the confessional.) Confessing an affair to your husband will absolutely ruin your marriage. Men never get over it. They will torture you forever. In addition, he'll feel entitled to pay you back in spades.

> Men are liars. We lie about lying if we have to.
>
> —JAY LENO

The Ultimate Fake Out

There is a lot more faking going on than there used to be, and it is not just happening with women! It is happening to women. Twenty-first-century liars, cheats, and opportunists have seized high technology as their partner in crime, and they are using it to con their way into or out of all kinds of situations as the perfect excuse, or the go-to alibi.

Let's take *Fake-A-Call* as an example. *Fake-A-Call* is an inexpensive iPhone application that allows you to not only fake a call, but to set the specifics of the fake call. The fake call can be set to a timer so that the call arrives at the perfect time, giving the emergency exit and the perfect "I've got to go" excuse. If spontaneous intervention is needed, just tap the "get ready to fake it" button, and the call will arrive momentarily.

This technology is like having a personal alibi on call 24/7. The fake call can even be programmed with a voice that can be played over the speakerphone. How terribly convenient for anyone getting the third degree to be interrupted by a call that is briefly put on speaker mode, so you hear the voice of the maitre' d from the restaurant (where he was pretending to be) say he left his credit card on the table. He then simply hits the mute button and carries on the rest of the conversation!

The layers of this deception can run even deeper by having the background of the call set to any desired image from the personal iPhoto library. To top it off, while programming this little hoax, the contacts button can be hit and instantly merge the alibi's information (like the 800 number for the chain restaurant) into the address book. This helpful little touch further backs up the cock-and-bull story upon late night cross-examination of the cell phone's call log. Talk about faking it!

Any guy who is prepared to fake a call is certainly prepared to use a *Fake Text* application to have his fake associate text confirmation of that suspicious Friday night business dinner.

Fake Text can be used as an alibi, an excuse or even as some phony information to impress you. It can even be used in dating (or business) as the instant qualifier, like having his private banker confirm the wire transfer, or having his fake assistant *Fake Text* a message not to cancel the Black American Express because he left it in the conference room (guess who is not picking up the bill for dinner!). Or perhaps he is upping his likelihood of getting lucky tonight after his buddy George Clooney confirms via *Fake Text* that he can stay at his house on Lake Como the week after Brad and Angie leave.

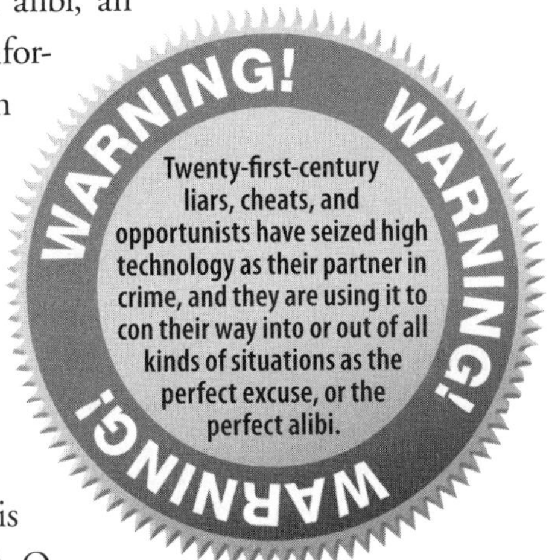

The high tech ways men are using to bamboozle their way into your heart, into your bed (or out of your bed), or into your bank account, are far too many to mention. These high tech tricks of deception may sound complicated. But guess what? All of these subversive programs and gadgets are ridiculously easy to use, and they are being used by **plenty** of men. I urge you to listen to your "gut feeling" and trust your intuition. Don't trust qualifications, evidence, or alibis just because of high-tech verification. Faking it the old-fashioned way seems minor league in comparison!

Why Men Leave

Men don't leave their wives unless another woman is waiting. They may cheat – but they don't leave! Women however, will leave their husbands when they're not "happy." Usually, they're not happy about their husband having another woman! But *why* do men leave? That's the real question. Sometimes the reasons men leave have nothing to do with their wives. It has to do with their immaturity, distractibility, issues with intimacy, lack of integrity or their own feelings of inadequacy.

If a man isn't happy with himself, then it's hard for him to be happy in a marriage. As a wife, you can only be your best self. You can't fix another person. Men who leave their wives don't *just* leave for better sex. Sex is only part of the equation. The other reasons are usually a compilation of complaints including lack of respect, nagging, criticizing, boredom and feeling underappreciated or taken for granted.

Men say things like the hot tamale they married now looks like an overstuffed burrito or that sex that used to sizzle has completely fizzled out. They begrudge when their wives haven't read a newspaper or walked a mile in ages. They resent when their wives are too tired to clean the house or make a decent dinner, yet somehow manage to find time to watch every episode of "Keeping Up With The Kardashians." **Men resent that the children get bedtime stories and they get bedtime excuses.** They resent that the woman they are now married to doesn't look anything like the one they said "I do" to.

The reason doesn't really matter. You can blame it on your baby, you can blame it on your hormone injections, you can blame it on your bloating, big bones, slipped disc, your thyroid, your slow metabolism, your love of cooking, Girl Scout Cookies, menopause, laziness or genetics. It doesn't really matter the reason. Your husband still notices the difference – even if he doesn't say anything. He notices. Even if he has let himself go – he notices. If you nag him more than you praise him –

he notices. If you don't listen to him – he notices. If you don't make him a priority – he notices. If you're not into sex with him – he notices. If you run around in sweats all day and go to bed wearing an old tee shirt – he notices. If he's not into sex with you, *you'd really better notice.*

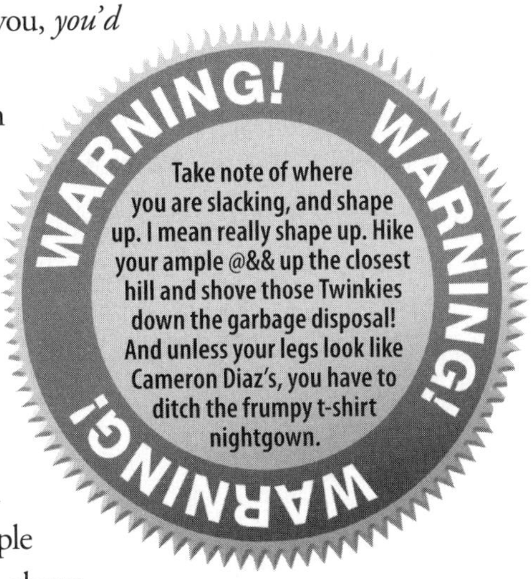

If this is ringing any bells with you, then I suggest *you* take a good look at your marriage and ask yourself this: **If your husband left you today, what would be the reasons he would blame on you?**

Take note of where you are slacking, and shape up. I mean really shape up. Hike your ample @&& up the closest hill and shove those Twinkies down the garbage disposal! And unless your legs look like Cameron Diaz's, you have to ditch the frumpy t-shirt nightgown. Stay current, and converse with him about what's going on in the world (not what's happening with Kris Jenner and the Kardashian girls!). Buy yourself some new lingerie. Show him that you're interested in what he has to say. Show him that you're a sensual, sexual woman who desires sex – with him. Make him a fabulous dinner and go with him on that fishing trip or to that baseball game. Build a life together that keeps him stimulated in healthy ways and has him too busy to run around looking for trouble.

Happily married men don't leave. Miserable married men don't leave their boring, nagging, overweight wives either – unless some Weed wiggles her way through the crack in the marriage and he follows her out the door.

Home-Wreckers 101

Every savvy wife should familiarize herself with the lesson plan outlined in the course guide for Home-Wreckers 101.

Lesson One: Weed targets a Stupid Vulnerable Husband (SVH). She flatters him, flirts with him, finds a way to establish herself as a prize and figures out a way to gain future access to him.

Lesson Two: Weed offers fantasy sex. She strokes his ego (along with a few other things) and feeds him the illusion of his idealized self. The ego-tripping combined with the adrenaline rush of secret sex makes for a highly addictive cocktail.

> WARNING! WARNING! WARNING!
>
> Weed targets a Stupid Vulnerable Husband (SVH). She flatters him, flirts with him, finds a way to establish herself as a prize and a way to gain future access to him.

Lesson Three: She combines frequent sex with emotionally engaging little fixes like email, poetry and secret telephone calls. When she has him under her spell, she gives a Meryl Streep performance, convincingly delivering the line: "I don't care about money. I love *you*."

Lesson Four: The Weed waits for the perfect timing (before he gets bored with *her*), and tips off the wife without having it look intentional. She may call and hang up in the middle of the night, drop earrings in his car, leave notes in his pocket, messages on his phone and email, scratches on his back or lipstick on his boxers.

Mid-Term: The wife reacts to the planted evidence and gives him the boot. Or, if the wife doesn't bounce him, then the Weed will do some extra credit work and resort to bolder tactics like writing her a letter, calling her directly or having her girlfriend reveal the affair to her. A Weed will not stop upping her antics until she feels certain to get results. A Weed is programmed to have no shame.

Final Exam: After the dalliance with the husband is brazenly shoved in the face of the wife, the Weed will be then be confident enough to prepare the loving sanctuary for the emotionally wrecked husband. The Weed will light the candles and chill the wine as she awaits his imminent arrival with the door open and her legs spread, thinking that soon your husband (and your life) will finally be hers! And she just might be right – unless the Stupid Vulnerable Husband is married to a Warrior Wife. In that case, the unworthy Weed will be exposed, humiliated and exterminated from both of your lives!

> "A Weed will not stop upping her antics until she feels certain to get results. A Weed is programmed to have no shame."

The Final Grade: The Weed will find out that in spite of wasting her time and giving her best effort, she has once again failed Home-Wreckers 101! The best grade she could get was an F – and we all know what that stands for!

The Weed will then have to start over with Lesson One. She will pull up her knickers, hike up her skirt, shoot up some Botox, and slither around the corner where she will wait until another Stupid Vulnerable Husband decides to indulge in the temptation of a piece of low-hanging fruit.

Love is a fire. But whether it is going to warm your hearth or burn down your house, you can never tell.

—JOAN CRAWFORD

Why Women Stay

Most women who get married do so believing they would never stay with a husband who cheated on them. Yet, life is full of surprises. Countless women end up doing the one thing they believed was impossible – they stayed married in spite of infidelity. The primary reason they stay is love – deep, complicated love. There are also plenty of practical reasons that have little to do with love:

> **Countless women end up doing the one thing they believed was impossible – they stayed married, in spite of infidelity.**

- Maybe she doesn't want to break up her family.
- Maybe she doesn't want some Weed trying to out-mother her or half-watch her children while their father watches football.
- Maybe she doesn't want her kids playing "step-parent ping-pong" and spending their lives in therapy.
- Maybe she can't afford to leave.
- Maybe she's waiting for her boyfriend to divorce.
- Maybe she hates having sex with him and couldn't care less about someone else taking care of that end of the business.
- Maybe she likes the gifts of remorse better than she likes her husband.
- Maybe she prefers having one underground Weed as the gatekeeper who closes the door on a bunch of others.
- Maybe she thinks he treats her and the kids better when he's cheating.
- Maybe she knows that without her 24/7 supervision, her children could grow up to be exactly like their idiot father.

- Maybe she would rather stay married and miserable than give her husband a shot at happiness with someone else.
- Maybe she thinks all men are the same, so she may as well keep the one she has.
- Maybe she saw what happened to her divorced girlfriends and doesn't want to be dropped from the dinner party list.
- Maybe her competitive spirit won't allow a Weed to win.
- Maybe she is waiting for her forensic accountants to finish their investigation so she can file for divorce and freeze the assets at the same time.
- Maybe she enjoys quiet revenge, watching Weed after Weed waste away their beauty years waiting for a man who will never leave his wife.
- Maybe she doesn't see a line of men waiting to take his place.
- Maybe she and her husband both have a "don't ask, don't tell the truth" relationship.

"The bottom line reason why a woman stays with a cheating husband: Because she has decided her life is better with him than without him – for now!"

The bottom line reason why a woman stays with a cheating husband: Because she has decided her life is better with him than without him – for now!

> Our greatest weakness lies in giving up. The most certain way to succeed is always to try just one more time.
>
> —THOMAS EDISON

How Women Stay with Cheating Husbands without Killing Them

Every wife who gets blindsided by infidelity will probably entertain more than a few crazed fantasies that involve committing a felony and a potentially successful plea of temporary insanity. Fortunately, most find a way to survive the experience and still stay out of prison. Some women punish their husbands with revenge shopping; others accept *peace offerings* like cars, clothes, jewelry, diamonds, flowers, fancy dinners and second honeymoons.

Many women consider diamonds to be a sparkling little sole and separate property nest egg to take with them if cheating happens again, which it certainly might. If a wife stays married after more cheating, then perhaps she has already decided she would rather keep the rest of her life as it is and stash away more diamonds while enjoying secret sex with a polo player instead of her rotten husband anyway!

Some women try strip classes or pole dancing in an attempt to put a new spark back into their old marriage. Others go to counseling. Some quietly build a lifeboat as they methodically plan their future escape. Some women stay and mark time with their philandering Casanova and hope that with a little luck, a few more steaks, a little blue pill and a couple martinis, nature may take care of the problem for her!

Even though most women don't readily talk about it, many, many women have found a way to survive the ordeal of infidelity and stay married. Most affairs end. If you don't push your husband out the door, he may never make a grand exit. If you're trying to come to terms with your difficult choice to stay married, the best advice is to continually remind yourself: **There is always dignity in family, and you choose to stay married because that's what's best for you and your family.**

Don't Serve Up Your Husband on a Silver Platter

So your husband cheated, your pride is hurt, your heart is broken and you think you should get divorced. You'd better be really, really sure before chucking away an otherwise good enough husband. Hold off on doing anything drastic, at least until you can think straight. Most women with children will tell you it was a big mistake to get divorced. Lifestyle changes, financial instability, disruption to the family, and unfathomable emotional stress make it worth doing everything possible to keep your marriage together.

Desperate Weeds spend years crawling around on their knees, hoping and waiting for an opportunity like this to close a deal with a brokenhearted husband who just got the boot. A Weed would love nothing more than to swiftly waltz your husband down the aisle while he's still dazed from the shock of you leaving him. This is the moment she's been waiting for!

Here is some wise advice from a powerful woman whose wisdom has saved many marriages: **I would not serve up my life up to anyone on a silver platter, and neither should you!**

Where's your competitive spirit? A Weed doesn't deserve to have your life just because she knows how to work a zipper! No way should you allow your husband to run off footloose and fancy-free with some Weed, leaving behind an emotional train wreck for your family. Oh no, he needs to be put under house arrest and endure his punishment like a real man! So snap out of it! Put on your Warrior Wife battle gear and fight for your family.

Yes, I know how hard it is, but just hang on to this little kernel of wisdom: **All men are jerks. God just gave them different faces so you could tell which one is yours!**

Peace Offerings

The time may come when your guy makes a mistake, a big one – the kind of deal-breaking mistake he knows you have no tolerance for. When you finally snap and pack his bags (or yours), he may panic and try to convince you how much he loves you and that the mistake will never happen again.

His remorse may be so great that he offers you a Kobe Bryant-sized "peace offering" if you will stay and give him another chance. But remember that offering is one thing, and making good on the offer is another. I know women who have learned both sides of this lesson.

One husband I know was so distraught about his wife's leaving him that he offered to put everything they owned in his wife's name if she would stay with him. Touched by his generosity, she stayed with him without making him follow through on the offer. So what happened? The only thing her husband learned was that he could talk himself out of anything. It wasn't long before he was up to no good again.

Another cheating husband offered his wife anything she wanted if she would stay. She said, "I want it all." She asked not out of greed, but because money matters big to men, and men understand financial penalty. Her husband agreed. They put together a new will, transferred all of their property assets to a life trust for her and their children, and made it irrevocable so that if he went back to his wayward ways, he would be the one in the doghouse and she and her children would continue living in the big house.

The bottom line is that if you allow your husband to make a big mistake and feel no pain, you're just asking for more trouble. If you take him up on an offer so generous it hurts, he's more likely to remember the lesson, and you're more likely to have his respect going forward.

Post-Traumatic Cheating Syndrome

Your marriage may survive infidelity, but don't think it'll be easy. The death of a spouse is actually easier for most women to get over. **Infidelity can cause feelings of loss, betrayal, humiliation and heartache that are so traumatic that you will have years or even decades in which you suffer from Post-Traumatic Cheating Syndrome.**

Post-Traumatic Cheating Syndrome can strike when you least expect it. You may be cruising along in your marriage when something suddenly triggers the memory of the infidelity, and you'll feel as if you're right back in the middle of the nightmare again.

The symptoms affect women in different ways. Some may plunge back into depression, some may burst into a fits of rage, some may hold their emotions and silently entertain visions of finding a pair of kitchen scissors and "going Bobbitt" on him while he sleeps, and some may feel they're selling their soul to the devil if they stay married another moment. Some women live for years on red-alert status keeping a bag packed in their trunk, a golf club in their hand and a divorce attorney on speed dial.

Post-Traumatic Cheating Syndrome is never one-hundred percent curable, but it's treatable, with symptoms lessening over time. What you don't want to do after coming so far in your marriage is to allow your Post-Traumatic Cheating Syndrome to drive your husband away. His guilty conscience may allow him to indulge your bastard-bashing binges for a while, but once he has shaped up and is toeing the line, his tolerance of your bashing will wane, and you may be the one put on notice to shape up and stop rubbing his face in the past, or he may elect to spend his future elsewhere.

Gratitude Journal

I am so grateful for the many blessings in my life. On this day I am grateful for …

TEAR OUT OR CUT ALONG LINE AND MAKE COPIES TO CREATE INSTANT GRATITUDE JOURNAL

WARNING! WARNING! WARNING!

DIVORCE

Is Your Marriage Doomed

There are a few ways to tell if a marriage is headed for divorce. Cheating, financial problems and abuse are obvious reasons, but the less obvious early indicator is contempt. Contempt is the equivalent of Mayday for a marriage.

Dr. John Gottman has been conducting studies with newlywed couples since the 1980s. After videotaping interactions of over 3,000 couples, Dr. Gottman was able to predict, with 90 percent accuracy, which couples would still be married fifteen years later. Couples who demonstrated contempt, either through speech or gesture, were the ones most likely to divorce.

How does one define "contempt?" Contempt takes everyday annoyance to another level. Contempt is demonstrated by scorn and condescension combined with a lack of remorse for bad behavior. When contempt becomes noticeable to the outside world, you're witnessing the disintegration of a marriage, whether you're aware of it or not.

"There are a few ways to tell if a marriage is headed for divorce. Cheating, financial problems and abuse are obvious reasons, but the less obvious, early indicator is contempt. Contempt is the equivalent of Mayday for a marriage."

If contempt has crept into your marriage, take heed and begin an emergency rescue plan. Don't dismiss this Mayday call, because the contempt you see and feel is only the tip of the iceberg; the power of its destruction is lurking beneath the surface.

I'm Not Happy

In America, everyone has the right to life, liberty, and the pursuit of happiness, but this pursuit should not be at the expense of your children's well-being. American families are in crisis because of selfish, self-involved adults who are pursuing their happiness with total disregard of what's in the best interest of their innocent children. Your pursuit of happiness can only be considered a noble cause if you take your husband and children with you.

To put it simply, "I'm not happy" is not a good enough reason to get divorced! Why should your happiness take precedence over your children's happiness? Once you have children, you have the moral obligation to take care of them and nurture them into adulthood.

As their mother, you cannot totally control the behavior of their genetically-challenged father, but you picked him, and had a child with him, so you're the one who has the obligation to try harder and figure out a way to make it work. You're the one who may have to sacrifice your pursuit of happiness for the happiness of your children. That's what a good mother does. She fiercely protects her children, and divorcing or choosing to be a single mother is not usually protecting them; rather, it is choosing to harm them.

Men may be the ones who are acting out, but women are the ones kicking them out and slamming the door shut on their families. The reason *why* doesn't matter to a child because the effect is the same when they don't have a father at home – sheer disaster! Children are never happy to have their fathers move out of their homes. Life without their father at home is a challenge they will struggle to overcome one way or another for the rest of their lives.

If you're married with children, your pursuit of happiness needs to take place within the confines of your home, family and marriage. Work it out.

Divorce Brings Out the Worst

Divorce brings out the worst in the best of men. It also brings out the worst in the best of women, so brace yourself if you're going down this road. You can get so caught up in the fight you become someone you don't even recognize. **No matter how wonderful (or terrible) your husband was during the marriage, you can be sure he will be even worse during the divorce.** You can expect him to try to manipulate you, both financially and emotionally. By the time it's over, you'll feel as if you've been through a war.

You always get more with honey than vinegar, at least in the initial phase. If possible, work out as many of the details of the agreement as you can before bringing your attorneys into the picture (including finances, custody, and personal rules of conduct with the children). The first settlement offered, while he's still wracked with guilt, is often the best offer and frequently better than the judge will give you.

Be smart about the specifics of your case and manage your attorneys. Remember, this is not their future they're negotiating; it's yours. The longer they can string out the proceedings, the better for them. To you, your divorce is about your family and your future. To your attorneys, your divorce is just a well-paying hourly job. The more you fight, the more they earn.

As for you, don't worry about being liked. No matter how nice you are, your husband will turn you into the enemy, at least until the settlement is over. You will have to fight hard just to get what's fair. Your standard of living is likely to significantly decline, while his will be higher within three years. Believe me, he will not hold back in doing what's best for him. You need to do the same.

They say when you first file for divorce you hate your husband, then you hate his attorney, and by the end of the divorce, you hate your attorney, too.

Hate Is a Four-Letter Word

When you harbor hatred (as women often do when going through a divorce), it doesn't hurt the person you hate! Hate only hurts the one doing the hating. Harboring hatred will harm you physically, mentally and emotionally. It will manifest into disease if you don't find a way to come to terms with your anger and release the pain. This doesn't mean spewing and venting to everyone around you. If you do this, you'll find that even friends will start avoiding you and your negative energy.

Find a way to forgive him for being the flawed, insecure, emotionally-challenged man he is. Dig deep and pardon him for lacking qualities like honesty, decency, integrity and compassion. When you release the bitterness and hatred from your heart, you can fill the space with love.

Whenever your mind wanders again into darkness, bring it back into light by remembering the things you're grateful for in your life. Say them out loud, keep a gratitude journal and write in it every night before you go to sleep. If you anchor yourself in a place of true gratitude, it will guide you in finding your way back to true happiness.

Forgiveness is a funny thing. It warms the heart and cools the sting.

—WILLIAM ARTHUR WARD

Children of Divorce

You may think divorce is the answer. Maybe it is for you, but unless your husband is physically or emotionally abusive, don't kid yourself into thinking it's good for your children. Not having two parents in the home is much worse than most parents realize. Divorce is not a single event for a child, but a series of traumatic events. Each detrimental consequence of divorce makes it more difficult for children to overcome hardships and grow up to be the happy, healthy, thriving members of society they were meant to be. The effect of divorce upon children is so serious that the emotional scars often carry with them into adulthood.

Children of divorce are almost twice as likely to live in poverty, have various behavioral problems and drop out of school. They have higher rates of suicide and depression. They have four times the risk of being plagued with obesity, drug addiction and alcoholism. They are more likely to commit a crime and end up in prison. They have sex earlier than children in two-parent homes and have more children out of wedlock.

Your children's futures will be greatly affected by your divorce. You owe it to your children to make decisions that are in their best interests, and getting divorced is rarely in their best interest.

When you have children, "I'm not happy" is not a good enough reason for divorce. So, until your "Plan B" for your family is far better than the "Plan A" you have now, you are probably better off to stick it out and try harder to work it out with your husband.

Your children deserve to live their lives without having to pay the price of their future for your divorce.

Guilty Father Syndrome

Being a stepmother is no easy gig, to say the least! For many women, being a stepmother is so difficult that they ultimately end up packing it in, not because of the stepchildren, but because their husband suffers from Guilty Father Syndrome.

Guilty Father Syndrome (GFS) occurs when a father feels so guilty about hurting his children and breaking apart the family that he becomes incapable of disciplining his children. **Fathers with Guilty Father Syndrome are so concerned with being liked by their children that they indulge their every whim and completely abdicate the enforcing of household rules or discipline.** It's also common for them to try to buy "favorite parent" status by overindulging them with things of a material nature.

Most stepmoms embrace their new kids in a sincere effort to create a great blended family. However, if she finds herself married to a man with Guilty Father Syndrome, she'll soon find that she's the only one doing the parenting. And instead of being thanked for it, she'll end up being resented. This causes the new stepmom to disconnect from her husband and disengage from the children.

The combined lack of engaged parenting causes the children to become spoiled, act out, and resist any and all authority and guidance. The situation usually gets worse over time and leads to bad grades, drug experimentation, and reckless promiscuity. Ultimately, the entire family suffers and the children pay the emotional price.

Guilty Father Syndrome is damaging for children and for marriages. Keep in mind, as a stepmother, the children's real issues – and loyalty – aren't with you, but with their biological parents. No matter how much you love them or care for them – you can give until the well runs dry - it will never be enough to compensate for what they don't get from their parents.

Blending a Family

The secret to a blended family is to start out on the right foot. Create a "parenting plan" that you and your husband can and will agree to follow. You must be on the same team in order to survive. Use the time prior to moving in to have a family meeting where you and your husband discuss what you expect from each other in terms of parenting. Cover topics like shouting, time-outs, warnings, cleanliness, homework, manners, bed times, discipline and consequences.

Two wildly different parenting styles are a disaster for blended families. Consult with a family counselor at this stage if your husband does not see the reason for clearly drawn rules of conduct.

Your husband must set the tone of respect if they are his children, and you must set the tone if they are yours. All of your children must have the same rules, even if you can't control what goes on when they go to the other parent's home. Resist the urge to allow them to play stepparent ping-pong when they don't like what you have to say. Bouncing from parent to parent should not be an option for your child. Adults should determine the schedule, not the children.

Remember that children (like husbands) need more praise than discipline. Be consistent. Let them know the rules and how they can expect to be disciplined if necessary. Also inspire them! Let them know how they will be rewarded for helping around the house, having good grades, and for good behavior.

Finally, don't talk negatively about their mother, and don't try to rub your status in the face of the ex by trying to out-mother her or by doing annoying things like sending them home with bottles of your perfume. If you start out strong and on the right foot, you can put together a happy blended family and avoid becoming a Stepmonster who reminds them of Joan Crawford in *Mommy Dearest.*

Helping Children Through a Divorce

If a divorce is inevitable, you have to rise above the drama. Work out an agreement with your ex regarding conduct and behavior that serves the best interests of your children. Reach this agreement while in the early stage of your divorce. If you wait until the war breaks out, then agreeing on anything is going to be difficult.

Losing dad on a daily basis is a huge loss for children. Try your best to keep your children in the same home and school. Don't discuss divorce details with them or in front of them. Work hard to keep yourself together physically and emotionally, no matter how difficult times may be. You have a responsibility to be strong in the eyes of your children (even if you aren't) so they continue to feel safe and secure.

Make it easy for their father to see them as much as he wants. It's very difficult for children to go back and forth trying to live in two different homes. If you give him as much access as he wants, he may not feel the need to go after joint custody.

Keep your children away from people you're dating until you're involved with someone you intend to marry. **Children of divorce have been destabilized enough; they need more of each parent, not a string of people coming in and out of their lives.**

And finally, stay close to your children! Make sure you communicate with them about their feelings. Stay involved with their lives and know what they're doing in school. Keep them involved in sports, clubs or activities. Know all of their friends and always keep their grandparents involved. Children have enough heartache with divorce, don't contribute any more by making poor parenting decisions.

It's a fact that your children will suffer because of your divorce. It's up to you and your ex-husband to determine how much or how little.

The Creation of Stepmonsters

Everyone hears stories of stepmonsters. Sometimes they're based on truth, and sometimes they're created as a coping mechanism for little children whose hearts have been ripped out by divorce.

A very articulate child of divorce once explained to me how her stepmonster came into her life. She said when she was about six years old, her parents separated, which was extremely traumatic and destabilizing for her. She hated going back and forth between the two homes. She said when she was with her mom, she missed her dad, and when she was with her dad, she missed her mom.

After a few years, her father married a terrific lady who was a wonderful stepmother. She said the problem was that every time she felt close to her stepmother, she felt like she was betraying her own mom. This anxiety made her feel so guilty it caused her to feel physically ill.

Then one day, quite by accident, she discovered that being angry with her stepmother allowed her to feel as if she was being loyal to her mother. That feeling was infinitely better than anxiety and guilt, so she created a fabricated negative image of her stepmother as a coping mechanism. She said she would try to find reasons not to like her. If her stepmother asked her to clean her room, she wouldn't speak to her for two weeks or until she forgot why she was supposed to be angry. Then whenever she started having feelings of affection for her stepmother, she would just find another reason to get angry and hold onto that until she forgot again. The cycle continued until she went to college.

Remember this story if you're a mother thinking of divorce or a stepmother who doesn't understand why your new husband's children don't like you. Most children don't know how to articulate the feelings of their broken hearts and the anger, anxiety, and betrayal caused by divorce. I urge you to consider what your grown-up decisions do to the emotional health of your children.

The Downgraded Divorcee

When you get divorced, you expect that people your husband knows through business would drop you as a friend. What you won't expect is that your friends (even ones that held your hand through the divorce) will drop you from their dinner party list.

Married women don't want divorced women around their husbands. Don't take it personally. They don't *necessarily* think you're going to go after their husbands. They just don't want the risk of having their newly single friend mixing and mingling with their husbands. Smart married women tend to enforce the No-Access Rule, even with their friends.

Another common reason is that many women have their own secret struggles with philandering husbands, and they prefer to keep it that way – a secret. Having a wolf for a husband is already private hell, but it would be far worse if he made a play for you too.

The truth is, some of your friends' husbands will make a pass at you. But why in the world would he think you would consider having sex with someone else's lousy, cheating husband when you just got rid of yours? I'll tell you why: Because men are such egocentric wonders, they really believe they stand a chance and are doing you a favor! No one is safer to cheat with than the wife's friend, except maybe the wife's sister!

Frankly, it is a no-win situation for you to hang out with your married friends anyway. You need to get serious about dating or, you're going to have some lonely nights and maybe even a lonely rest-of-your-life. All of this doesn't mean your friends don't cherish you. It just means you're temporarily downgraded into the category of the single friend, the lunchtime friend, girl's dinner friend, telephone friend, but mostly a "find your own guy and stay away from my husband until you do" kind of friend!

Ponder

What would you attempt to do if you knew you would not fail?

—DR. ROBERT SCHULLER

Our deepest fear is not that we are inadequate. Our deepest fear is that we are powerful beyond measure. It is our light not our darkness that frightens us. We ask ourselves 'who am I to be brilliant, gorgeous, talented and fabulous?' Actually, who are you not to be? You are a child of God. Your playing small doesn't serve the world. There's nothing enlightened about shrinking so that other people won't feel insecure around you. We were born to make manifest the glory of God that is within us. It's not just in some of us; it's in everyone. And as we let our own light shine, we unconsciously give other people permission to do the same. As we are liberated from our own fear, our presence automatically liberates others.

—MARIANNE WILLIAMSON

Keep away from people who try to belittle your ambitions. Small people always do that, but the really great make you feel that you, too, can become great.

—MARK TWAIN

Take the first step in faith. You don't have to see the whole staircase, just take the first step.

—DR. MARTIN LUTHER KING JR.

"This is the beginning of a new day. You have been given this day to use as you will. You can waste it or use it for good. What you do today is important because you are exchanging a day of your life for it. When tomorrow comes, this day will be gone forever; in its place is something that you have left behind . . . let it be something good."

—AUTHOR UNKNOWN

WARNING! WARNING! WARNING!

I WILL SURVIVE

When the Going Gets Rough

In life, not all days are going to be sunny. Sometimes the darkness falls upon us all when real life hits us square in the heart with pain, loss, frustration, disappointment, weight gain, new wrinkles, flat tires or some other despair. At some point, everyone wants to dive under the covers and hide from the rest of the world – but what's the point? Hiding doesn't help anything. All you're doing is wasting your most precious commodity – the days of your life. So when the going gets rough, drag yourself out of bed, get dressed, and put on your makeup. And no, I'm not kidding. The darker the days, the brighter the makeup you need to wear!

On dark days, it's important you muster the energy to make yourself look good. Otherwise, you'll find yourself in deeper trouble when you look in the mirror and see that you look the way you feel. The sun will come out again, but you won't know it if you stay under the covers. So get out of bed, put on your makeup and go out and face the world!

Everyday Success

It's important you start and finish something every day, preferably in the morning. Completing a task, no matter how small, has a way of validating your competency, energizing you spirit and lining you up for success for the rest of the day.

The task doesn't have to be difficult. Clean out a drawer, recycle your magazines, write a long-overdue thank-you note or call someone you love and tell them how much they mean to you. Every task completed gives you the feeling of success and helps align you with positive energy for the rest of the day.

Mending a Broken Heart

Some relationships are meant to be – just not meant to be forever. If you're brokenhearted, experience the pain and cry your eyes out, but not for more than a few days. Be grateful for the experience and for what you learned. Remind yourself that you know you're not destined to be in this world alone. There is someone for everyone.

This is your one and only life. Time is precious, and reliving the past does you no good. Neither does wasting too much time mourning. Write down everything you learned from this relationship and how you feel about the experience in your *Bad Dog Journal.* Get it out, learn from it, and then let it go. It's behind you now. Close the book, and take one step forward. You're not mourning what you lost! You're mourning the loss of what you hoped it would be.

This is no time for destructive behavior. This is the time to get in shape for the rest of your life! You need your strength and your health. You need to eat food that nourishes your body as you find a way to heal your soul. Exercise every day, even if you start with just a thirty-minute walk. Complete a little project every day. Do something nice for someone else every day. Read inspirational books before you go to sleep. Be grateful you have another chance to get it right! You can't change the past, but you can create your future, so be kind to yourself and embrace the process of creating a future you really deserve.

If you can't swing out of it on your own, then get a recommendation for a cognitive therapist to help you learn positive ways of moving forward. You don't need to dwell in the past; you need to learn how to live in the present so that you can love in the future.

Leaving Your Comfort Zone

We are all on our own journey, and at this moment you're standing where your journey has taken you. Even if you would like to forget some of your past experiences, you can still appreciate the lessons you've learned. Read some of the books from the very wise Dr. Wayne Dyer, who teaches us that there are no accidents in life. Each experience we have, no matter how painful, eventually leads us to something of higher value. When you look back, you'll see that everything made sense and is part of an unfolding plan.

From this point on, wherever you go and how you lead your life is your choice. All possibilities are in front of you. If you choose, you can change your life and your destiny. Don't use past failures as an excuse not to try again. Go on a self-help mission of exploration. **Ask yourself the famous Byron Katie question, "Who would you be without your story?" and learn to get on with your life and leave your story behind.** Pick up the books of Anthony Robbins, the self-help titan who teaches, "Change happens in an instant of decision" and how you too can change your future with one decision. Seismic changes in a single life can happen in an instant – sometimes in the blink of an eye – so decide what you want to do and find a way to do it! It's that simple! Don't let fear stop you, because that's your past talking.

Take one small step toward tomorrow today. You'll find it's not as hard as you imagined. A new path is always uncomfortable. Use the discomfort to drive you, knowing it symbolizes your courage in the face of a new adventure. As long as you're committed to arriving at your new destination, don't worry about the detours along the way. It's all part of the process! If you're relentless, and continue steadily moving forward, you'll get where you are going. Don't ever let a setback keep you from getting back on the road to your dreams.

Looking for Mr. Right

If you're ready to get serious about finding Mr. Right (again), then it's time to think about your re-entry into the dating world. You'll feel better about starting over if you love the way you look. It gives you confidence, changes your energy, and sends out a signal to men that you're desirable.

Men are primitive creatures guided by primal radar. Most men will take one look at you, and the desire to sleep with you will either register or not. Their primal radar tells them if you're a potential mate or just a buddy. And by the way, men will gladly sleep with a willing buddy, but a potential mate needs to immediately register on the primal radar. Like it or not, first impressions are extremely important! When you're ready, and you look good and feel good, men will come out of the woodwork to be around you. You never know where you'll meet the love of your life, so make a point of looking good no matter what you're doing.

Don't expect to find the love of your life in bars. Oh, he might be there, but alcohol has a way of making it hard to tell Mr. Right from Mr. One-Night-Only. Instead, go to art openings, museums, lectures or the farmer's market. Go to the movies on Wednesday nights (a great night for meeting divorced dads with their kids). Take classes, join study groups, or take travel tours. Get involved in a political campaign or, better yet, volunteer for a charity or go to the obvious places – football, basketball or baseball games.

If you're a child of the digital age, check out some of the online dating services and "speed dating" groups in your area. Most importantly, have fun! Men love the energy of women who love what they're doing. Remember, years go by quickly and there's nothing better than finding the love of your life. If you stay out and about, the love of your life might just find you.

Patterns of Destruction

Pain has a short memory. Thank goodness! Humans would experience little joy in life if pain stayed in the front of our consciousness forever. The downside is that the same survival mechanism that allows us to forget also makes us vulnerable to repeating the same mistakes over and over.

Are you one of the many women whose relationships all seem to have the same dysfunctional storyline, just played with a different leading man? If so, you're destined to continue living a life trapped in your own pattern of destruction unless you make some drastic changes. If you want to learn from your mistakes instead of continually reliving them, then you first must evaluate your dating history.

Begin by creating a Bad Dog Journal where you'll write down the details of your entire dating history. No revisionist history either! Spill it all. Where did you meet? When did you sleep with him? Why did you decide to sleep with him? How long did it last? What were your conflicts? When did you know the relationship wasn't going to last? What lies were told? What were your mistakes in judgment? What caused the breakup? When did you know he was wrong for you? What was dysfunctional? What did you do wrong? What commonalities do the men have? What did you learn? Leave nothing to the imagination!

Read, study and analyze your relationship patterns, remembering that you can't change a pattern unless you realize one exists. Keeping a Bad Dog Journal allows you to remember what you shouldn't forget. Otherwise, time will pass and you'll once again forget about the details, the hardships and the lessons you had to learn so painfully. If you study your patterns, you'll learn how you can change the ending of the story from tragedy to "happily ever after."

TEAR OUT OR CUT ALONG LINE AND MAKE COPIES TO CREATE INSTANT BAD DOG JOURNAL

Bad Dog Journal

Date: ______________________________

Name of Dog: ______________________________

Incident: ______________________________

____

____

What did I learn? ______________________________

____

____

____

____

Advice to Self: ______________________________

____

____

____

____

____

____

____

____

Incident Rank Prince 1 2 3 4 5 6 7 8 9 10 Dog

Looking Right for Mr. Right

Showing you care about your appearance is a clear signal you're interested in attracting men. Men will choose a woman of slightly lesser beauty with great "style" over a woman who may be more beautiful but has bad hair, unstylish clothes, a chipped tooth or poorly applied makeup. Before you start looking for love (or even a new job), get some expert advice and treat yourself to a makeover. You may think you don't need one, but do it anyway. It's difficult for women to be objective about their style and the way they look.

Don't rely on opinions of your friends. They may be too kind, too brutal, or take offense if you don't listen to their suggestions. And truth be told, they may not want to help you look more fabulous than they do! This is why we ask experts. Create an inspiration book of makeup, fashion, style and hair you admire from your favorite fashion magazines, and then meet with experts. Go to a high-end department store and consult with their personal shopper. Ask their makeup artist to give you a current look and teach you how to do your own makeup. These services are free at the major department stores.

Every city has its superstars for beauty. (In Los Angeles, it's Negin Zand and Tracey Cunningham for hair color, Salon Cristophe and Nick Chavez for cut, Dr. Mark Friedman for a movie star smile, Sylvie Levy Lemay for cosmetic dermatology procedures, JJ Virgin for Weight Loss Resistance, and Carrie Wiatt for Diet Designs.) Make it part of your mission to find out the best of the best in the city you live in and schedule a consultation. If you let the experts know your mission and that you're open to change, they'll probably tell you the truth about what needs to be done. Once you trust the advice to be right for you, go for it and enjoy looking like your best self!

Remember, men like conquest and they like to win; if you want him to feel like he hit the jackpot, you have to look like the prize!

Back on the Merry-Go-Round

So, you're dating again? Good! Just know you may have to kiss (or speed date) a few toads before you find your Prince Charming. Here are a few useful tips to remember when sitting down at the audition table:

- Don't bore him with the details of your last breakup.
- Don't tell him you want to get married again.
- Don't talk about all the men you're dating or not dating.
- Don't whine about your financial situation.
- Don't torture him with tales of your everyday drama.
- Don't dress like a nun – or a hooker.
- Don't try to be smarter than he is in his area of expertise.
- Don't talk about tragedy of any sort.
- Don't talk about the doom and gloom of the economy.
- Don't talk about religion, psychics or politics.
- Don't do all the talking!

Relax, smile and enjoy yourself! There is something to learn from every dating experience. Be enchanting, be interesting – and be interested in him. Remember that a sense of humor goes a long way in life. Consider ending the date a little on the early side while your energy level is still high. It's better to leave him wanting more. A little mystery is always good thing.

Listen closely to what he has to say because it may tell you what you need to know about him. Don't invest too much emotional energy in wondering if he'll call again. Just keep busy and keep dating. If you're not desperate, you won't seem desperate. Keep your dance card full and keep dancing until someone sweeps you off your feet.

Listen Up

When you're on a date, remember this: Men love to talk about themselves, so pay close attention to what they have to say. In the first few dates, men will usually tell you what you need to know – both good and bad.

Sometimes a man will show his stripes with obvious slips like, "Men are not meant to be monogamous," or "My ex keeps taking me to court over child support," or jokes "What happens in Vegas stays in Vegas, right?" The flipside is you might hear remarks like, "I'm so ready to be a father," or "I sent my mom on a cruise with four of her girlfriends," or "My brother and I just got back from a Dodger game with my sister's children." These little "tells" will let you know if you have a reason to even bother with a second date.

> **"In the first few dates, men will usually tell you what you need to know—both good and bad."**

Either way, relaxing over a simple dinner is often the best way to sneak a peek at his true character. Don't dismiss what you hear. Write the details of your dating experiences in your Bad Dog Journal. If you document your dates over the course of a month, your notes will start to add up, and you'll get a good indication whether he has the makings of a champion or if he's just another Bad Dog in disguise.

Luck

They say the definition of luck is "when preparation meets opportunity." In other words, you have to make your own luck! Don't wait for great things to happen. Make things happen. It only looks like luck to other people.

Gratitude

Begin every day by asking yourself "What am I grateful for?" This simple, little ritual of observing the blessings in your life helps set the tone of your energy for the day. You'll be a happier person if you stay in a constant mindset of gratitude.

Most people don't really understand that you can't fake energy. Your personal energy is your truth. If you feel anxious, worried, depressed, angry, sad, stressed or frustrated, that will be the energy that emanates from you no matter what you think. It doesn't matter how much you want something, how much you believe you can have it, or how much you chant about what you want to attract into your life, if your energy is not in sync with your desire, it won't happen.

Remember this: Your personal energy will always override your intention. That's the real secret to *The Secret.* It's also the real secret as to why *The Secret* doesn't work for most people. You can't fake energy.

The simplest way to change your energy is by being happy, and the easiest way to shift into a state of happiness is by consciously shifting into a place of immense gratitude for all of your many blessings. If everyone you love is healthy and you're not dealing with tragedy, then you have no excuse for not staying in a continual place of gratitude. When you feel love and gratitude, you're not only emanating energy that can attract your desires, but you're also changing the energy in your body into that of health and healing.

Have fun, be grateful, live your life with the optimism of Forrest Gump and remember, "Don't worry, be happy." That's the real secret of *The Secret.*

Don't Worry About Perfection

The universe has a way of helping your dreams manifest into reality if you stay in a place of gratitude and focus on what you want in life, rather than on what you "don't want" or "don't have."

If you don't worry about being perfect, you'll find you can accomplish a great deal more in life. Setting perfection as your only acceptable standard can immobilize you. If you do nothing, you'll get nothing. There must be energy expended to create forward motion. If you want your dreams to come true, then focus your energy and follow through with the action required. Just do it. The universe likes speed.

Remember, you never get more than you ask for.

Time Passes No Matter What You Do

Your greatest commodity in life is how you spend your time – so spend it doing things that are meaningful with people you respect. Days, weeks and years melt away very quickly. In this fleeting life we have on earth, it's best if you never lose sight of the passage of time, because you can rest assured Father Time never loses sight of you. The clock is ticking away your life right now. What are you going to do?

I say, live your life with gusto! Stay present in every moment. Don't wait for your life to happen. It's your life, nobody else's, and it's only here once. It's happening right now – in this and every moment. If you want to know if you'll be happy in the future, ask yourself if you're happy right now. If not, don't waste another minute. It's time to change your tomorrow today.

Forgiveness

There is great power in forgiveness. Releasing anger and hatred lightens your soul. If you let your past stay in the past, then it won't dominate your future. You don't have to be friends with people you've had issues with, but you will be happier if you don't think of them as enemies. Think of them as teachers.

Work to accept and understand that people are flawed, and everyone is on their own life journey doing the best they can with the circumstances that surround them.

> **"Work to accept and understand that people are flawed, and everyone is on their own life journey doing the best they can with the circumstances that surround them."**

You will be much happier and healthier if you practice forgiveness. Forgive yourself, forgive others, and go forward on your own adventurous journey with warmth and compassion in your heart.

How Can It Be Better?

Talking and dwelling on what went wrong in a situation is demoralizing for everyone. Instead of focusing on the negative, try reframing the dialogue into a positive exercise asking, "How can it be better?" This change in mindset will make all the difference in the world to the people around you. Take it upon yourself to help motivate others to go forward and do a better job next time. Inspiration always brings about better results than criticism.

Play Ball Like the Big Boys

This is the time in your life to aim high and go after what you want. Unfortunately "going for it" doesn't come naturally for a lot of women.

For most women, in order to have the courage to ask for something big, we first have to check the alignment of the stars, step on the scales, check our horoscope and make sure we have a good hair day. If everything adds up, maybe we'll go for it. If not, we'll wait until the stars line up again and everything else is in check.

> **"For most women, in order to have the courage to ask for something big, we first have to check the alignment of the stars, step on the scales, check our horoscope and make sure we have a good hair day."**

Men have none of these worries. When men want something, they ask for it without giving second thought to their hair, weight or the weather. And if they get a "no," they just keep asking until they get a "yes." My theory is that all those years of team sports prepares boys to become men able to cope with striking out under pressure and getting right back up to bat the next inning.

Women have to learn to do the same thing. Just take a deep breath and go for it. What do you have to lose? If you strike out, get back up to bat. Keep swinging until you get the "yes" you're looking for. That's how you play ball and win in the game of life!

> A real decision is measured by the fact that you've taken a new action. If there's no action, you haven't truly decided.
>
> —TONY ROBBINS

You Blew It

There is nothing worse than wrecking your life by your own hand. Even if you've made the mistake of all mistakes, you still have to find a way to come to terms with it and forgive yourself for doing something truly stupid. It won't be easy.

The first step is to vow to never make such a mistake again. Then, do your best to fix the situation. Don't worry about your pride. Show them how much you care. Humble yourself and apologize, then apologize again. Send a thoughtful gift or their favorite chocolates or something else you know they love, and then apologize one more time.

Our capacity for forgiveness is greater when someone demonstrates sincere remorse and shows they care enough to try to remedy the situation. Do the best you can, and if nothing works, at least you know you gave it your all. If you can't fix the damage you've done, then you must let it go, and forgive yourself anyway.

Vow to be a better person and get on with your life. You haven't lived if you haven't made a few mistakes. These experiences challenge us to grow, and let's face it – some lessons are destined to be learned the hard way.

When people tell me they've learned from experience, I tell them the trick is to learn from other people's experience.

—WARREN BUFFETT

Depression

If you're really depressed, you first need to find out if it's chemical, circumstantial or both. (Read *The Depression Answer Book* by Wes Burgess, M.D., Ph.D.) Never stay in a state of severe depression for long without seeking help. Get a professional diagnosis. Sometimes medication can correct a chemical imbalance, and that will be enough to lift the grey clouds of doom.

There are also a few basic steps you can try on your own that may help you swing out of it. First of all, make sure you are eating properly. Good nutrition can make a world of difference. Also, exercising daily can help. It's amazing what even twenty hard minutes of morning exercise can do for your spirits. If you're still not feeling better, get your Vitamin D level checked by your doctor, because a deficiency is very common in women, and that is often linked to depression and Fibromyalgia. Fifteen minutes of direct sun is good for your bones and good for your soul!

Unfortunately, the circumstances of your life may be such that you have good reason to be depressed; however, you still can't indulge in depression for long. You need to change what's not working in your life or come to terms with what you cannot change. It is healthy to acknowledge the events that caused your depression, but don't dwell on them. Pain will linger if you look at it too long.

Focus your energy on the present! Pull yourself together and stop doing anything even remotely self-destructive. It's important to change your mental outlook and retrain your brain to focus on what you want in your life, not on what's missing. Move forward with your life and read or listen to motivational or inspirational programs until their wisdom inspires you to take charge of your life.

Finally, get out and engage in the present day and the world around you. The sun always shines again, even after the darkest storm!

The Rx Rollercoaster

It may have started with a backache, a broken bone, anxiety, panic attacks or a migraine. Your doctor gives you a prescription for Xanax, Valium, Vicodin or some other miracle in a bottle; it eases the pain, and it works, perhaps a little too well. Before you know it, you're reaching for the bottle when your greatest stress is getting the children off to school or getting to the gym.

It's easy to find yourself living in denial about your addiction as you and your doctor work together to fight off the symptoms of your mysterious illness with an ever-changing prescription drug cocktail. Most of the time, your debilitating illness is actually your body suffering symptoms of the withdrawal, or the side effects of the increasing dependency.

Everyone around a prescription drug addict knows all the reasons they cite as they cling to their diagnosis and the *necessity* of taking their medication. If you're one of these women, you aren't fooling anyone. The people around you know you have a prescription drug problem. They know you need help. They also know you distance yourself from them and shut them out when they get anywhere near the subject of addiction with you. So they wait, hoping you don't die or hit rock-bottom before you decide to seek help.

Your loved ones can't want sobriety for you more than you want it for yourself. Only you can help yourself by admitting you are powerless over your addiction. How do you know if you're powerless over your addiction? If you could quit on your own, you would have done it by now.

You must be the one to make the decision to take your life back. Go to an AA meeting or check into rehab for a supervised detox. You are only Twelve Steps away from having your health and your life back. It will be well worth the effort when you do.

An Affair with the Bottle

You'd be surprised how many "successful" women have a secret affair with alcohol. They never intended it to happen. The seduction started gradually – just a little wine with lunch and maybe a martini at dinner to soothe away the worries of the day. It was so natural to make drinking a part of daily life.

How do you know if you're having an inappropriate affair with the bottle? Here is an indicator: If you drink during the day and you're not celebrating a birthday, then you're probably an alcoholic.

> **"How do you know if you're having an inappropriate affair with the bottle? Here is an indicator: If you drink during the day and you're not celebrating a birthday, then you probably are an alcoholic."**

Alcoholism takes a toll on a woman's health, her life, her looks and her family. Women are forced to hide the truth when the bottle takes priority over the needs of the family. Time after time, they try to end the affair, only to succumb to a physical and psychological hold that won't let go.

If you're trapped in this kind of affair, know that it can cost you your life. If you want to save your life and your family, stop living in denial! Accept that you're powerless over this addiction and seek help. The fact is, if you could have stopped drinking, you would have stopped drinking!

Go to an Alcoholics Anonymous meeting and start with the first step. You can stop drinking, but you can't stop alone. You'll have to endure a one-day-at-a-time death match in order to break it off. It won't be easy, but if you don't win this battle, you'll die.

Alcohol is an abusive partner that will never willingly let you go.

The Stepford Life

One of the things you learn when you get older is that people are not living the Stepford lives you thought they were. It turns out, whether they throw stones or not, most people live in glass houses. They pretend to have perfect marriages, faithful spouses, plenty of money, great sex, perfect children, healthy eating habits, zero addictions, no hot flashes and of course, no need for Viagra. Sometimes it's true; sometimes it's true for a while; and sometimes it's the furthest thing from the truth!

Eventually, some unexpected event like an affair, addiction, bankruptcy, mental issues, foreclosures or lawsuits will break their glass house and expose the truth inside. Exposure is a devastating experience, especially for the Stepford people who have managed to convince themselves they really were the perfect family.

Something profound happens to Stepford people when their glass house gets broken and the truth inside is exposed. It may take the Stepford's time to face the world again, but most eventually do, and that's when they realize great change has taken place. Former Stepford people often come out from the shattered glass feeling stronger than ever once they realize they've survived the catastrophe; the world is still round, and they no longer care what "everyone" thinks. They still have family and friends who love them and have gained a new appreciation for what really matters in life.

When the Stepford illusion is gone, they can still live with the fact that the world is flawed, people are flawed, and everyone is doing the best they can with what they've got, and life is still worth living! Oh, don't get me wrong though, for the Stepford life is a glorious way to live – if only it were real!

Famous Beauties on Beauty

"Beauty can get a woman what she wants: love and money. But when beauty leaves you, so can the things it bought."

—PAULINA PORIZKOVA

I look forward to being older, when what you look like become less and less an issue and what you are is the point.

—SUSAN SARANDON.

For years I stopped reading beauty magazines because I couldn't look at one without wanting to blow my brains out. How can those women look so good?

—JAMIE LEE CURTIS

Plain women know more about men than beautiful ones do.

—KATHARINE HEPBURN

The problem with beauty is that it's like being born rich and getting poorer.

—JOAN COLLINS

I think if I weren't so beautiful, maybe I would have more character.

—JERRY HALL

People see you as an object, not as a person, and they project a set of expectations on to you. People who don't have it think beauty is a blessing, but actually it sets you apart."

—CANDICE BERGEN

The average man is more interested in a woman who is interested in him than he is in a woman with beautiful legs.

—MARLENE DIETRICH

Beauty is how you feel inside, and it reflects in your eyes. It is not something physical.

—SOPHIA LOREN

WARNING! WARNING! WARNING!

BEAUTY & AGING

How Much Fake Does It Take?

If you have decided to try to fake your way to the best breasts money can buy, then here is a little something to keep in mind before you go the Dolly Parton route. When it comes to the bigger is better philosophy of breasts, *most* guys prefer that if you are going to fake it, you at least try to fake it well enough so the size could be theoretically real. How big is too big?

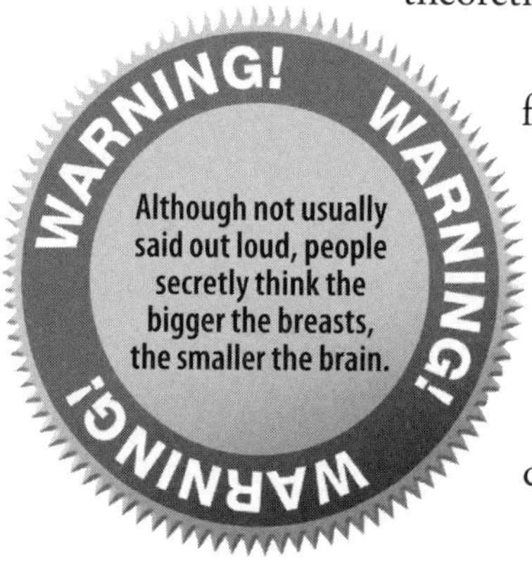

That answer really depends. Are they for a stripper pole or marriage? Certainly there is no shortage of single women sporting stripper-size double Ds, and men certainly notice stripper size double Ds. They'll readily hop in the sack with them, but they generally don't marry them.

Most people think there's something a little off with women who buy giant, fake breasts. (Dolly Parton is the one and only exception). And most women think there is a little something off with men who desire fake breasts that are larger than bowling balls. Although not usually said out loud, people secretly think the bigger the breasts, the smaller the brain. To most, *giant* fake breasts symbolize promiscuity, instability and low self-esteem. It seems when it comes to a wife, men prefer theirs not to look like a hooker.

I have a lot of married friends, and not one wife sports stripper-size double D's. Except, of course, those who are sporting double chins too!

Cougar Barbie

We all see women who have lost perspective when it comes to turning back time – faces too tight, eyebrows too high, breasts too fake, lips too big. Unfortunately for them, these women don't seem to have a clue that others are whispering behind their backs.

Most women don't realize what they're doing to themselves. One of the most obvious mistakes happens with lips. Just because women *can* make their lips bigger doesn't mean they *should.* Yet they keep going back for more, and they don't seem to notice something that may have started out as a good thing has gradually gone terribly wrong. Maybe it's because women look directly into the doctor's mirror and don't realize that in profile, their new lips make them look like a distant relative of Daisy Duck!

Here's a hint: If your face has been injected so much that it looks like a blowfish ready to explode, maybe it is time to stop bragging about never having a facelift! There is only so much you can do this side of a scapel.

You have to be very careful about doing too much too soon, because if people can tell you've had work done, they often assume you must be *older* than you actually are. Otherwise, why would you have so much work done so early? What a nightmare! Women can put up a good fight, but it's hard to win in a battle with age. Be sympathetic. Not one of those "fountain of youth" chasing women you notice with bad plastic surgery or overblown, frozen faces ever thought it would go wrong, and she would end up looking as frightening as The Joker from Batman, with her smile permanently stretched from ear to ear.

When it comes to plastic surgery and cosmetic enhancement, proceed with an abundance of caution. **It's better to look a little older than to look like a freakish Cougar Barbie before you're fifty!**

Gotta Get My Groove Back

If you feel like you're fat, then maybe you are! It doesn't matter if you're already married to the love of your life, men generally prefer women who are fit – not fat. If you want to lose weight but are stuck losing the same pounds over and over again, then maybe I can help, as I have successfully coached women in losing weight they thought would never go away.

I'm not a fan of most diets because all the rules create ongoing feelings of deprivation, which, in turn, create negative energy that permeates throughout the rest of your life and leads right back to rebound pounds. I have two plans that work, each requiring only one simple change in the way you eat and the way you think. Before you start, clear it with your doctor, as I have no nutritional qualifications whatsoever – just an impressive track record.

Serenity Diet – Start every morning with the Serenity Prayer: "*God grant me the serenity to accept the things I cannot change, the courage to change the things I can, and the wisdom to know the difference.*" Then say to yourself, "I can eat anything I choose, and every other day I choose to eat only fruit." Then do it. One simple change. No other rules.

Snow White Diet – You can eat anything you want as long as it's not white. Nothing white means no white ingredients such as flour, sugar, rice, pasta, white bread, potatoes, burger buns, fries, pizza, cookies, pancakes, donuts, chips, or basically anything processed. You say to yourself: "I can eat *anything* I want, and I choose not to eat anything white."

Both of these formulas work. Don't watch the scale. Just stay with the program until you get your groove back. How will you know how much is enough? My advice: Don't stop until you feel like dancing naked on the tabletop!

The Brazilian Bush

Are you hairy high and low? When you take a trip down under, does it look like you need a ticket for a jungle cruise? Or is your hair so long that if you comb it, it looks like the head of your childhood Troll Doll? We all love long, beautiful hair – just not down there! Getting rid of pubic hair drives women crazy: shaving, waxing, depilatories, ingrown hairs and stubble. It's never-ending aggravation. You can learn many things about a woman by her method of hair removal.

A weekly waxing means she's still into sex. Summer waxing means she likes to look good in a swimsuit, but sex at home is bread and butter. Au natural (no waxing, no shaving, no nothing) may be used as a form of birth control for the impulsive, or may simply indicate a secure natural woman. Shaving means a sensible and practical woman. The Full Monty Brazilian with no hair *anywhere* means she wants you to think she's young, hot, and over sexed – even if she's not! Hair (or lack of it) is so revealing!

Fortunately, science has blessed women with a way to end our hairy worries once and for all, and that's the Brazilian laser. Now you can permanently zap your unwanted hair into any shape you want (bikini, triangle, strip, stripe, heart, or totally bare). No more pain, stubble, in-grown hairs, or smelly, stinging hair remover. It's also one sure way to take care of grey hair down there! It's a little pricey, but many women find it to be money well spent not to have to deal with the nuisance of unwanted hair.

A word of caution. There is no such thing as defying gravity. Everything continues to go south as we age. Baring down to The Full Monty may not be the best look at sixty! If you decide to do something permanent, hedge a little both ways. Tell them to clean the garage area and let the pyramid point the way!

Little Cracks and Creases

Here is another little secret for a more youthful appearance. It's called StriVectin SD. This product was invented to shrink and reduce stretch marks and has been found to reduce facial wrinkles. It seems this external cream gets results almost *anywhere* you have tiny wrinkles. A word of caution, this treatment is strictly word of mouth, and I don't suppose StriVectin will be printing *those* before and after photographs!

Limp Lobes

They say you can tell a woman's true age by her earlobes, or the scars next to them! It's hard to enjoy wearing fabulous, attention-getting earrings when you see what they look like on limp, droopy earlobes. Here is another secret women don't talk about: They get their dermatologist to plump up their earlobes with a shot of a filler product like Restylane.

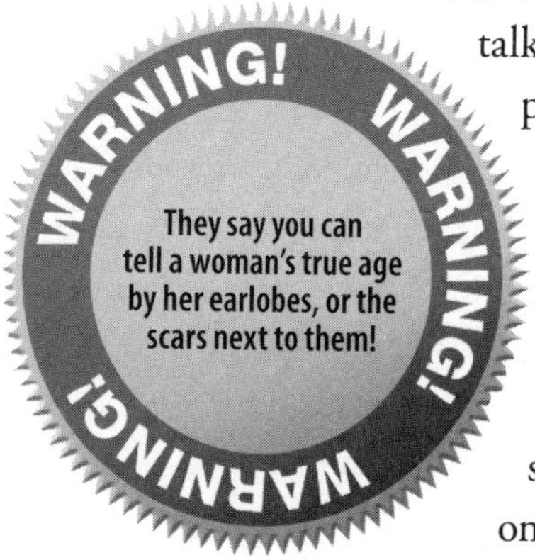

Now any aging beauty can have plump, youthful-looking earlobes to show off beautiful earrings or perhaps entice a little nibble on the ear from someone who still nibbles. If it were only so easy to plump up *everything else* that goes droopy under the evil hands of time!

> You'd be surprised how much it costs to look this cheap!
>
> —DOLLY PARTON

Pretty Privates

As time goes by, every southern landscape loses its majesty. With numerous border crossings and the delivery of a few large bundles of joy, the changed landscape can make some women feel so inhibited that any traveling south of the border can only be done with the lights out on the darkest nights.

If you have long, irregular, or over stretched inner labia, and the embarrassment or discomfort interferes with your life and causes you to have a low self-esteem and a poor genital self-image, then you should check out the DVD *Viva la Vulva* to see a real variety of what real women's genitals look like. Odds are yours are perfectly normal. You just have to stop comparing yourself to the airbrushed women in magazines.

However, if that doesn't do it and you really are suffering, then Labiaplasty may be something to look in to. It's a minor surgery that trims and reshapes the external appearance of the labia, giving a more youthful appearance.

If you think this minor surgery is what you have been waiting for, then do your research and go to a certified plastic surgeon who has a lot of experience. Ask to see his before-and-after photos. A doctor who does plenty of these surgeries will have photographs for you to see.

You don't have to live your life suffering in silence with a genital self-image that is so poor and debilitating you feel forced to keep your privates way too private. This minor surgery could transform you from wanting to do nothing more than bumping uglies in the dark to hoping Tommy Lee is going to show up with his video camera!

Where's My Libido

Are you wondering how women are supposed to manage in this over-sexed world when you're expected to bring home the bacon, take care of children, prepare the meals, do the laundry and turn into a lusty sex goddess every time the lights go out? What can a woman do to rev up a burnt-out libido so that sex is something you look forward to instead of the last thing on your to-do list?

Women still don't have the equivalent of the little blue miracle in a bottle. And why would they, considering the pharmaceutical companies and the insurance companies are industries dominated by men! There are, however, a few solutions that work for some women. The first thing to try is to kick up your exercise and shift to a low-carbohydrate diet, increasing your consumption of salmon and tuna. Simple as it sounds, these changes often do the trick.

"What can a woman do to rev up a burnt-out libido so that sex is something you look forward to instead of the last thing on your to-do list?"

Some women whose libidos have taken a permanent hike have been thrilled with the effects of hormone replacement therapy. HRT is usually a combination of estrogen, progesterone, and a little kick of testosterone. There is still controversy surrounding the long-term effects of HRT, so it's best to use it as your last resort rather than your first.

There are also holistic alternatives that offer hope. The first is called Xzite. It's a mixture of Chinese herbs first tested at the UCLA Medical Center. Xzite claims that 73 percent of women participating in the trial reported increased satisfaction with their sex lives. It's recommended by sex experts Drs. Jennifer and Laura Berman, as well as actress Suzanne Somers. I have a friend who is the wife of a prominent doctor, and she told me she takes it late in the afternoon and can't wait to get her husband of twenty years in bed the minute he gets home. Twenty years with same guy! Must be good stuff!

The other is called Arginmax, a multivitamin and herbal mix that includes ginseng, ginkgo, damiana (a South American herbal aphrodisiac) and L-arginine (an amino acid that plays an important role in sex). Arginmax was studied at Stanford and received favorable results. Both products are available online. Before you take any medication or supplements, check with your doctor and do your research. And when you find that your sex drive comes back, I hope it comes back for your husband and not your handyman or pool boy!

Pretty in Pink

If you peer down south one day and notice "things" are getting a little dark, dingy and gray, it might be time to take action and get you back in the pink. Try a little age spot cream or a mild skin lightening cream with Hydroquinone. Test a little to make sure you don't have sensitivity to it, then use some every few days until you lighten up to where you want to be. It will get you back in the pink in no time!

> If God wanted us to be naked, why did he invent sexy lingerie?
>
> —SHANNEN DOHERTY

Beyond Kegels

After years of enjoying hot sex and having a couple of little darlings to show for it, you may find something other than your jaw line needs a little tightening. If you have a large problem in that neighborhood that goes far beyond anything Kegels will correct, then maybe Vaginoplasty may be a solution you should know about. Let me be clear: I am not suggesting or recommending this surgery. In fact, I think it's a terrible idea to be messing around with a knife in this neighborhood. This may be a solution to consider, but only if there is a *giant* problem that is ruining your life. Certainly you shouldn't consider this for the sake of vanity.

Vaginoplasty is a surgery that cuts the vagina to make it smaller and tighter. This is done to increase friction during sex and give greater sensation to both partners. Beware. I've heard of this particular surgery going terribly wrong and ruining everything that used to work perfectly well. The surgery can tighten up the neighborhood up to such a degree that it is painful to accommodate anything larger than a pencil stick, or you may find out that a slight repositioning throws everything out of alignment. This is one area where you're certainly not going to get a recommendation from a girlfriend (they are all as snug as Stepford virgins), so you'll have to do your own extensive research to find a great doctor.

This is an extreme surgery that you should not even consider unless you feel it's absolutely necessary. You certainly don't want to risk mutilating your body for some guy who read about Designer Vaginas in a men's magazine! This surgery may make for titillating storylines in magazines and shows like *Nip/Tuck,* but the reality is that any surgery can be dangerous. PROCEED WITH CAUTION! If everything is in good working order, why risk ruining something good by trying to fix something that isn't broken?

Manopause

As men age, they begin losing testosterone. This natural testosterone decline is similar to the hormonal drop that women experience as they grow older, but it happens more gradually in men. **Some women call this male-menopause, some call it andropause, some call it manopause, and some just call it relief!**

Manopause may cause men to become nicer and more sensitive; however, some men experience more extreme symptoms like fatigue, depression, anger, anxiety, memory loss, lack of sex drive and erectile dysfunction. Viagra may not be the simple solution if he is depressed and has no sexual desire in the first place.

If your husband's Manopause is interfering with his life, or if you're considering trading in your old man for a raging bull, you may want to help him out. Encourage him to try increasing exercise, losing extra weight and cutting back on alcohol. If those don't do the trick, you can send him to his doctor and get his hormone levels checked. His doctor may be able to kick him back in gear with a combination of supplements and hormone replacement therapy.

Before you decide to fix his Manopause, consider this: If you help him get back in the game, he may surprise you and turn into a player who starts playing the field. Keeping that in mind, you have a few options of your own to consider. You can let nature takes its course, and let sleeping dogs lie. You can lie to the sleeping dog and take your raging hormones elsewhere. You can take your chances, and let his doctor give him a miraculous testosterone-laced secret potion and enjoy having your own Benjamin Button, who once again can perform like a man twenty years younger. **Or, the best option may be just keep your mouth shut about Manopause, find yourself a rocking chair, and hit the power button on your Magic Wand!**

The Wrinkles in Your Future

In your twenties, you have no idea how you're going to age. All the youth and beauty you take for granted when you're young will fade as the years go by. Father Time is not known for being kind to women, and you never know who will age well and who won't. Sometimes that unique beauty that made you so cute in your twenties turns into something other than cute in your thirties or forties. In your twenties, just being young is beautiful enough for most men.

Unfortunately, no matter who you are, somewhere in your thirties you get slapped with a dose of reality. You wake up one day and realize no matter what you do, how much you spend, or what tools and techniques you use, you're still not going to look young. The best you can hope for as years go by is that you look good for your age. And just because you hope to look good for your age doesn't mean you actually will!

> **"Sometimes that unique beauty that made you so cute in your twenties turns into something other than cute in your thirties or forties. In your twenties, just being young is beautiful enough for most men."**

My point is, if you're in your twenties or early thirties, don't underestimate youth as one of your best assets. Realize what a great hand you've been dealt, and play your cards early. It may not be a winning hand if you hold your cards too long. Aging is a bitch we all meet too soon!

> The world's biggest power is the youth and beauty of a woman.
>
> —CHANAKYA

Now You Know

After reading *The Real Secrets Women Only Whisper,* you have just learned the secrets millions of women have had to learn the hard way. My hope is that you'll be a quick study and that you can learn from the mistakes of others and bypass having to learn so many lessons the hard way.

The 21st century has brought with it enormous challenges for women to deal with and overcome. It is time women band together to elevate the world around us for the benefit of our future and our children's future. I believe all women have a story to tell and wisdom to share. If you use any of the advice in this book and find it helpful, please share your story with other women at TheRealSecretsWOW.com.

Obviously after reading this book you can see why it is best to keep it out of the hands of men. So mark the pages you want handy reference to, and then hide this book away. We certainly don't need to give men any ideas they don't already have!

Just know that when it comes to men, you can do everything right and still get no lifetime guarantee. But if you follow my advice, you will at least have a better chance of stacking the odds for success – or at least survival!

The goal is that when you turn forty, fifty or even sixty, you'll be able to sit back and say, "Thank goodness I listened" instead of whispering to a friend, "If I only knew then what I know now . . . "

The next best thing to being wise oneself is to live in a circle of those who are.

—C. S. LEWIS

20/20 Hindsight

What have *you* learned on your journey? Starting now...

✷ I will try to stay in a place of gratitude for the many blessings in my life.

✷ I will listen to my intuition.

✷ I will forgive myself – and try to forgive others.

✷ I will take the time to share my wisdom with other women.

✷ I will be mindful to...

✷

✷

✷

✷

✷

✷

✷

Sources and Additional Resources

SOURCES CITED

Alcoholics Anonymous. *Twelve Steps and Twelve Traditions* (AA World Services, Inc., 2002).

Angelou, Maya. http://www.mayaangelou.com/ (May 14, 2009) and http://thinkexist.com/quotation/i_don-t_know_if_i_continue-even_today-always/9187.html (May 14, 2009).

Behrendt, Greg and Liz Tuccillo. *He's Just Not that Into You: The No-Excuses Truth to Understanding Guys* (Simon Spotlight Entertainment, 2006).

Cosby, Bill. "Address at the NAACP on the 50th Anniversary of Brown v. Board of Education." Constitution Hall, Washington D.C. 12 May 2004. http://www.americanrhetoric.com/speeches/billcosbypoundcakespeech.htm (May 14, 2009).

Coulter, Ann. *Guilty: Liberal "Victims" and Their Assault on America.* (Crown Forum, 2009).

Dunstan, Priscilla J. "Dunstan Baby Language," http://dunstanbaby.com/ (May 14, 2009).

Gottman, Dr. John. "Love Lab Studies at the University of Washington, 1994." http://www.gottman.com/ (May 14, 2009).

Hrdy, Sarah Blaffer. *The Woman that Never Evolved* (Harvard University Press, 1999).

Jung, Carl. *Modern Man in Search of a Soul.* (Mariner Books, 1955).

Katie, Byron. *Who Would You Be Without Your Story?* (Hay House, 2008).

Onassis, Jacqueline Kennedy. http://www.whitehouse.gov/about/first_ladies/jacquelinekennedy/ (May 14, 2009).

Robbins, Anthony. *Awaken the Giant Within: How to Take Immediate Control of Your Mental, Emotional, Physical and Financial Destiny!* (Free Press, 1992) and http://www.tonyrobbins.com/home/home.aspx (May 14, 2009).

RECOMMENDED READING, VIEWING & LISTENING

- *Twelve Steps and Twelve Traditions* by Alcoholics Anonymous, AA World Services, Inc., February 10, 2002, ISBN 0916856291
- *He's Just Not That Into You: The No-Excuses Truth to Understanding Guys* by Greg Behrendt and Liz Tuccillo, Simon Spotlight Entertainment, December 26, 2006, ISBN 141694740X

- *The Depression Answer Book: Professional Answers to More than 275 Critical Questions about Medication, Therapy, Support, and More* by Wes Burgess, Sourcebooks Trade, May 1, 2009, ISBN 1402217129
- *Make Money, Not Excuses: Wake Up, Take Charge, and Overcome Your Financial Fears Forever* by Jean Chatzky, Three Rivers Press, March 11, 2008, ISBN 0307341534
- *Living History* by Hillary Rodham Clinton, March 31, 2004, ISBN 0743222253
- *Come On People: On the Path from Victims to Victors* by Bill Cosby and Alvin Poussaint, Thomas Nelson, October 9, 2007, ISBN 1595550925
- *Child Sense: From Birth to Age 5, How to Use the 5 Senses to Make Sleeping Eating, Dressing, and Other everyday Activities Easier While Strengthening Your Bond with Child* by Priscilla Dunstan, Bantam, October 27, 2009, ISBN 055380667X
- *Excuses Begone!: How to Change Lifelong, Self-Defeating Thinking Habits* by Wayne W. Dyer, Hay House, May 26, 2009, ISBN 1401921736
- *Supernanny: How to Get the Best from Your Children* by Jo Frost, Hyperion, January 12, 2005, ISBN 1401308104
- *Not "Just Friends": Rebuilding Trust and Recovering Your Sanity after Infidelity* by Shirley P. Glass, Free Press, February 3, 2004, ISBN 0743225503
- *Ten Lessons to Transform Your Marriage: America's Love Lab Experts Share their Strategies for Strengthening Your Relationship* by John M. Gottman, Jullie Schwartz Gottman, and Joan Declaire, Three Rivers Press, June 26, 2007, ISBN 1400050197
- *The Woman That Never Evolved* by Sarah Blaffer Hardy, Harvard University Press, December 20, 1999, ISBN 0674955390
- *On Becoming Fearless...in Love, Work, and Life* by Arianna Huffington, Little, Brown and Company, April 9, 2007, ISBN 0316166820
- *Who Moved My Cheese? An Amazing Way to Deal with Change in Your Work and in Your Life* by Spencer Johnson, G.P. Putnam's Sons, September 8, 1998, ISBN 0399144463
- *Who Would You Be without Your Story? Dialogues with Byron Katie* by Byron Katie, Hay House, October 15, 2008, ISBN 1401921795
- *Women & Money: Owning the Power to Control Your Destiny* by Suze Orman, Spiegel & Grau, February 27, 2007, ISBN0385519311
- *Awaken the Giant Within: How to Take Immediate Control of Your Mental, Emotional, Physical, and Financial Destiny!* by Anthony Robbins, Free Press, November 1, 1992, ISBN 0671791540

- What's Your Self Worth? By Dr. Cheryl Saban, Hay House, May 2009, ISBN 978-1-4019-2395-2
- *Your Best Life Now* by Joel Osteen, Warner Faith, Time Warner Book Group, October 2004, ISBN 0-446-53275-4
- *Soul Series* by Oprah Winfrey, http://www.oprah.com/oradiohost/oss
- *Act Like A Lady - Think Like A Man* by Steve Harvey, Harper Collins Publishers, 2009, ISBN978-0-06-172897-6

PRODUCTS & SERVICES

The Real Secrets Women Only Whisper, www.TheRealSecretsWOW.com
Soul Series by Oprah Winfrey, http://www.oprah.com/oradiohost/oss
XM/Sirius Satellite Radio, http://www.xmradio.com
Cedar's Sinai Medical Center C.O.A.C.H. for Kids, http://www.csmc.edu/3591.html
Victoria's Secret Lingerie and Intimate Apparel, http://www.victoriassecret.com
Hitachi Magic Wand Personal Massager, https://secure.themagicwandshop.com/cgi-bin/UCEditor?MERCHANTID=MWS&ThemeCode-Store
The Rabbit Personal Massager, www.therabbitvibrator.com
Trojan Vibrating Touch, www.vibratingtouch.com
California Pizza Kitchen Restaurant, http://www.cpk.com
E-Blaster Internet Tracking Software, http://www.e-blaster.com
KeyKatcher Mini Device Internet Tracking Software, http://keykatcher.com/
Fingercam, The World's Smallest Wireless Camera, http://spytekohio.com/index.php?main_page=product_info&products_id=99
SpectorSoft Internet Tracking Software, http://www.spectorsoft.com/
Loopt, http://www.loopt.com/
Google Mobile Latitude http://www.google.com/mobile/default/latitude.html
National Network of Private Investigators, http://www.411investigate.com/
Check Mate Semen Detection Test, http://www.getcheckmate.com/
Children's Health Fund, http://www.ChildrensHealthFund.org
Xzite Herbal Female Sexual Enhancement Formula, http://xzite.org/
Arginmax Sexual Enhancement Formulas for Men and Women, http://www.arginmax.com

Index

T

U

V